LEARN & USE
LINUX
MADE EASY

MAXWELL COOTER AND
DAVID CARTWRIGHT

FLAME TREE
PUBLISHING

CONTENTS

For those who are brand new to Linux, this chapter will offer you an introduction to what it is and everything it has to offer. We'll explain why Linux is one of the best operating systems currently available, and explore how it compares to others such as Mac OS and Windows. Any questions you may have about choosing Linux can be answered here.

This chapter discusses the importance of the Linux ecosystem and will help you get to grips with the basics behind it. You will learn valuable information on what a distro is, explore the main vendors and decide which would be most suitable for you. We'll also compare and contrast the various shell families including sh/ksh/bash vs csh and tcsh.

GETTING STARTED

Here, you will learn everything you need to know about getting started with Linux. From suggesting what you should be looking out for, to providing help and support on downloading the chosen distro of your choice, this chapter will be able to help with any queries you may have.

WORKING WITH LINUX

This chapter will really help you get to grips with everything there is to know about actually working with Linux. We'll provide informative guides to the many different distros: Ubuntu, Debian and Red Hat etc., as well as compare the similarities and differences between them. For those planning to create or download a range of files, we will offer advice on what storage system would suit you best.

LINUX AND SECURITY

Staying safe online is incredibly important to us, and so this chapter will provide you with enough information to ensure your safety. With advice on Linux firewalls and helpful information on wireless security settings, your Linux system should remain safe from any nasty surprises.

LINUX AND NETWORKING

For support and advice on how to get connected with Linux, this chapter will guide you through the necessary steps to do so. We'll teach you how to set up your wireless network as well as explore telnet and port configuration in more detail.

LINUX AS A SERVER

For those who are unsure how to go about setting up a Linux server, look no further. This chapter will show you how to configure a personal NAS (Network Attached Storage), as well as how to use the Apache web server. It also includes step-by-step guides on how to generate self-signed security certificates.

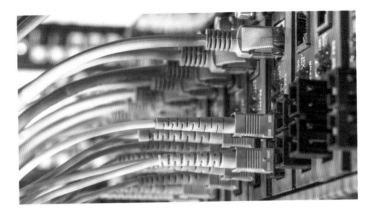

TROUBLESHOOTING & GLOSSARY

Often things do not go smoothly, and so when those times occur, we have the solutions. In this chapter, we will try to provide the best solutions to any problems you may have as well as offer all the technical terms you may need.

INTRODUCTION

Starting out with Linux can be difficult, especially if you're brand new to the sometimes complicated operating system. This guide tells you everything you need to know to get started, from the very basics to some of the more advanced capabilities of Linux.

ABOUT THIS BOOK

This is a book about Linux: if you're a hardcore Linux user who's used to arguing the merits of Debian against Fedora, it's not for you. If you're a professional IT person already managing an Apache web server, it's not for you ... but if you're interested in an adaptable, flexible and efficient operating system and want to know how to get the best from it, this book is most definitely for you.

While it's true that you can buy into Linux by going through a commercial distribution (distro) or by using a partner, it's far more fun and interesting if you do it all yourself. Yes, there's a lot to learn and you'll have to get to grips with the notion of the Linux shell and the demands of a command-line interface, but this book will guide you.

WHAT CAN YOU EXPECT?

In the first chapter, you'll learn about the history of Linux: who Linus Torvalds is; the philosophy behind free and open-source software; and why so many developers devoted their time to getting services off the ground. While this won't help you become a Linux expert, you will understand some of the rationale behind the operating system and why there are so many distros about.

THE HEART OF THE OPERATING SYSTEM

Chapter two is about Linux itself and the supporting ecosystem. It takes us to the heart of the operating system and helps you understand how Linux is structured: what's in the kernel and what's in the shell (see page 44).

There's also much more detail about the various Linux distros, what the main ones offer and how they differ. There's plenty of information to help you choose the right one.

Then we finally get to some of the technical differences as we examine the various shell families and compare the shells sh, ksh and bash to csh and tcsh (see page 68) – this may seem like a return to algebra lessons, but it will become clear what they all mean. In short, each one of them gives you the ability to write configuration files that set up Linux the way you want.

CHOOSING YOUR DISTRO

Then we get to chapter three. This is where we really get started with Linux. We now come to the nitty-gritty of downloading your chosen distro (see page 52). They're not all the same and there are step-by-step guides to follow to make sure that you can get your chosen distro up and running properly. Screenshots alongside the step-by-step guides will ensure that everything is easy to follow so you can set up your Linux the way you want.

What Programs are Available?

There's also a look at what programs you can run with your distro. For example, if you want to select an email system, there are plenty to choose from. How do you decide between Postfix and Sendmail, for example? We look at what to consider when deciding which one is best for you.

IN-DEPTH DETAILS

You can get further information on how the different distros work in chapter four (see page 60). This time, we go into the detail of how they all work and pick up on their idiosyncrasies and foibles. All of them have their pluses and minuses, and it's important to know these. Hot Tip boxes placed alongside the text give you that extra bit of advice that can make all the difference.

SECURITY

One of the most important aspects of an operating system is security. There's been plenty of debate about how secure Windows is and the ways that Microsoft has looked to beef up the safety of its own operating system. A Linux machine is considerably more secure, but that does not mean that security should be ignored.

In chapter five, we take an in-depth look at all aspects of Linux security, with a detailed examination of secure remote log-in facility – SSH – how to use it and what you should be looking out for.

Linux Firewalls

There's more to this chapter than SSH; it also looks at how to provision and administer Linux firewalls and goes into detail about wireless security, an essential part of any modern IT user's armoury.

SETTING UP YOUR CONNECTION

Computers don't usually work in isolation, so chapter six examines how a user can establish a Linux connection. The chapter will take into account both wired and wireless connectivity – looking at everything you need to know about Linux networking.

LINUX AS A WEB SERVER

You may well be interested in using Linux as a server. In this case, you'll be interested in chapter seven. This goes into much more detail about what you'll need to do to establish a viable Linux server and how to configure a personal NAS (Network Attached Storage) server (*see* page 214).

Apache Web Severs

We also get to grips with one of the major uses of Linux: how it is used to drive Apache web servers. This is one of the areas where Linux really does hold sway over its competitors: about two-thirds of web servers across the world are based on Apache.

If you're going to be using Linux as a web server, then you're going to have to learn about how to generate self-signed security certificates and how to run SSL-protected websites. Chapter eight shows you how.

TROUBLESHOOTING

After that, we have the very important troubleshooting section. This tells you how to fix some common problems. We look at what to do when you can't log on remotely, what to do when you lose the connection, and the value of a decent back-up. This chapter essentially explains the importance of not sawing through the branch you're sitting on!

There's also a complete glossary, so you're not left baffled by any terms that you come across on your Linux journey.

THE START OF YOUR LINUX JOURNEY

Within the space of a couple of hundred pages, it's impossible to cover the full range and richness of Linux. There are so many distros out there, each with their own advantages, that there's something for everyone; we can only push you in the right direction. There are plenty of resources out there that can take you further, and there are plenty of people to help you. One of the joys of Linux is that everything's out in the open and everything is geared towards collaboration. If you have a query, someone is going to be able to answer it. This book will get you started: how far you go is really up to you.

Hot Tip

As you go through this book, look out for Hot Tip boxes, for getting even more out of your Linux experience. From extra resources to insights learned from decades of using Linux, these tips will start you on your way to becoming a Linux expert.

INTRODUCING LINUX

WHAT IS LINUX?

So, you want to use Linux. Congratulations, you have selected an operating system that will offer so much more than traditional operating systems when it comes to security, reliability and interoperability. You have selected an operating system that drives many of the servers that power the internet today and that provides the basis for many of the current, fast-growing cloud computing market.

While it may be new to you, Linux is everywhere. It's the operating system that's at the heart of Android phones, the most popular smartphone technology today. It serves as the basis for Google's Chromebooks. Have you got a TiVo? Guess what operating system lies within the TV

Below: Linux drives the home of the CERN Large Hadron Collider.   © CERN

Hot Tip

The bootloader is the software that boots up the operating system, so it is a vital part of Linux. For most people, it is the screen they see before the operating system loads.

recording device? Do you use a sat-nav to get around? TomTom is a Linux product too. And if you wonder what technology lies at the centre of the CERN Large Hadron Collider, wonder no more: it's Linux.

BUSINESS TURNS TO LINUX

But it's not just in the hidden manifestations: it's a technology that's very much in demand within the IT workforce. According to the latest report from The Linux Foundation, nearly 97 per cent of organizations are currently looking to hire professionals with Linux skills, with salaries sky-rocketing accordingly.

That's the way that business is going: this situation is a reflection of how many organizations are running Linux-based servers. It's a technology that is fast-growing and is set to catch up with existing Microsoft-based servers – hence the demand for the professionals to run them.

Linux Around the World

We've already seen some large-scale Linux deployments across the world. Both the New York and London stock exchanges use Linux for their trading platforms. It's an operating system used within banks, schools and local authorities across the globe.

Right: Linux is used in many vital businesses around the world, including the New York Stock Exchange.

A UNIQUE ALTERNATIVE

But while the business world is increasingly turning to Linux, the desktop market is different. Those very same enterprises are still running desktops on Windows (not forgetting the increasing use of smartphones and tablets within the business world) and Linux won't be getting much of a look-in.

It's futile to pretend that you're buying into an operating system that is wildly popular. Linux, in all its manifestations, has less than three per cent of the desktop market – nothing like enough to make serious waves. But, as all its many supporters will tell you, what you are choosing is an operating system that is richer, more flexible, more secure and more efficient than its Microsoft and Apple counterparts. And, of course, being free is another big bonus.

This book will look at some of these advantages, going into a bit more detail about Linux's strengths and why it scores over its commercial competitors.

NOT ONE BUT MANY

There should be a little explanation, here: when we say operating system, we are being slightly disingenuous. Linux isn't one operating system, but several. Linux is based on a single kernel with a multitude of different providers offering different functions in the vast range of other components that are switched with it.

This book will look at some of the major offerings (or distros – short for distributions) and how they differ. One of the beauties of Linux is that, as opposed to Microsoft Windows or Mac OS, you're not given a one-size-fits-all chunk of software, but one that can be adapted for your own particular needs. If you're new to Linux, you may well want to try Ubuntu or Mint (which is a variant of Ubuntu, just as Ubuntu is a variant of Debian).

Below: Ubuntu, one of the leading Linux distros.

LINUX DOWNSIDES

There have been some controversies surrounding Linux. One of the most widely heralded Linux contracts was when the City of Munich decided to switch from Windows to Linux back in 2003. It started to move 4,000 desktops to a distro called LiMux, but things didn't quite work out as expected, and five years later, there'd only been an adoption rate of 20 per cent. Eventually, the target desktops were all migrated, just in time for the deputy mayor to announce that the city was thinking of switching back to Microsoft.

There were two issues at the heart of this decision. One of these was the cost of supporting Linux. As mentioned earlier, there's a bit of a shortage of skilled Linux developers at the moment, so working with Linux is a lot more expensive than working with Microsoft. It's true that all the major Linux vendors will offer in-house support – and there are vast forums to call on – but if you need hardcore Linux techies, they are going to be more expensive than their Microsoft counterparts.

Compatability

The other problem with the Linux implementation in Munich was the lack of operability with existing Microsoft programs, both within the city and with other German local authorities. It should be stressed that, as yet, there's been no decision as to whether Linux will be ditched, but the arguments about the roll-out show that there are still a lot of issues. Munich isn't alone, other local authorities have looked to move to Linux only to draw back (Bristol City Council investigated the possibility only to decide to stick with the status quo). They all face the problem of a lack of Linux developers and problems with operability with existing applications.

A HUGE VARIETY

Another problem with Linux is the number of distros. This makes it tough to make the right choice. What doesn't help is that each distro has its own supporting cast of fanboys and asking 100 Linux users for their opinion would quite possibly elicit 100 different responses, each person pushing forward his or her favourite. It's not an entirely personal preference: there are some scattered examples where a product doesn't work with one Linux distro but will work with another. It doesn't happen often, but there are some slight oddities around.

Linux Programmers

The fact that Linux is open and that there's plenty of opportunity for discussion is normally presented as an advantage for the operating system, but it can be a disadvantage too. There can be conflicting pieces of advice given and it's not always easy to sort out the useful advice from the unwanted. There have also been instances when developers have got sidetracked into areas that are interesting for programming challenges but not so useful for users. The likes of Microsoft and Apple will task their programmers with solving real user challenges to offer features that are useful (not always successfully, it must be said). Linux programmers may well be more interested in solving technical problems.

But these are minor issues when it comes to home users. For most people, Linux offers a world of new experiences and an opportunity to move away from the limitations of Windows.

Hot Tip

Confused by the many different distro options? You can check the top 100 on the Distrowatch website: distrowatch.com

LINUX HISTORY

Linux didn't appear out of nowhere and it's useful to examine how the software came into being. This is because that history has a bearing on how the operating system is perceived today and why some companies and individuals, who would normally be expected to be sympathetic, have issues with Linux.

There's a philosophy driving Linux: a collaborative, sharing movement. This has been a reaction against the use of proprietary software (the likes of Microsoft or Apple). It's important to realize that Linux isn't out on a limb, here there are plenty of other similar initiatives – it's just that Linux is the one with the most visible presence.

Below: The GNU operating system was one of the first examples of a free software project.

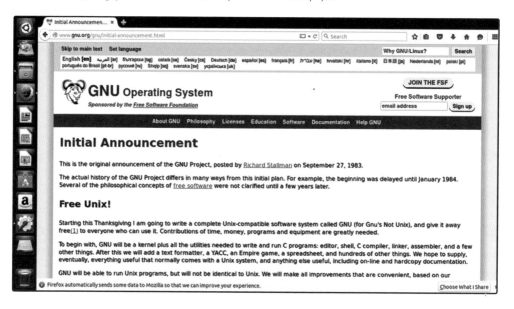

The roots of the operating system lie in the free software movement of the 1980s. One of the leading lights of this was a programmer called Richard Stallman who, in 1984, set up the GNU Project, which in turn led to the Free Software Foundation the following year. In this case, 'free' is free as in politics, not free as in beer (to use the usual analogy).

PRINCIPLES OF FREEDOM

The idea behind this freedom was to give computers more power to share information, a collaboration that would lead to improved performance. Under this concept of freedom, users had the power to study the underlying code, poke around with it as they wished and modify it accordingly. One of the important aspects of this development was a new type of software licence – the GNU General Public Licence (GPL), which instead of the usual copyright restrictions, operated under 'copyleft' guidelines.

The General Public Licence

This type of licence, developed by Stallman, not only ensures that software is free to be modified, but that these rights are retained even after modification. In other words, this means that an individual or organization cannot take free software, modify it and use that modification for proprietary purposes – once free, always free.

The GNU Project was all about developing a completely new type of operating system, one that operated under these free principles. It was into this world that Linux was born: it was developed using GNU tools and released under the terms of the GPL.

OPEN SOURCE

One term that you will often hear bandied about is open source. This phrase stems from about the same time as the free software movement was getting underway. It started when two other programmers, Eric Raymond and Bruce Perens, founded yet another free software movement, one they called the Open Source Initiative (OSI).

The emergence of OSI was due to a political split among free software advocates: between those who opted for the concept because it led to better programs and those who thought there was something intrinsically worthwhile about free software. To a certain extent, these rows continue to this day – there are various strands of opinion about what open source and free software mean.

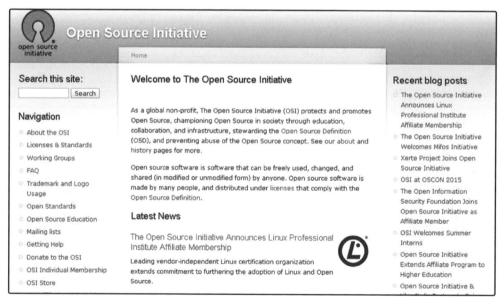

Above: The Open Source Initiative: the start of a new movement in software development.

FREE AND OPEN SOURCE SOFTWARE

The discussion has led to the creation of a portmanteau phrase – free and open source software (FOSS), a sort of compromise between the two strands of thought. In reality, there's already a strong overlap between the two and some of the differences between the two schools are of the same arcane nature as those of medieval philosophers arguing about the sex of angels. Some of the arguments touch on all aspects of life – they're not just technical issues (and they fall well outside the scope of this book). For most people outside this world, the two are interchangeable, but if you're talking with software developers, don't be surprised if they take a more nuanced view.

The Cathedral and the Bazaar

If you want to learn more about these schools of thought, a very good introduction is Eric Raymond's book *The Cathedral and the Bazaar*. This draws a distinction between the two approaches. There's the GNU way (the cathedral) where a small group of developers work together in secret, presenting their work at the end of the project, and the Linux way (the bazaar) where the code is developed in public, with many people contributing to the success. From this, Raymond derived Linus's Law: 'Given enough eyeballs, all bugs are shallow' or, to put it another way, 'Many hands make light work'.

THE DEVELOPMENT OF LINUX

That's the history of the free software movement, now it's time to look at how Linux itself emerged. While one of the strengths of Linux is the number of people who contribute to the code, just one man working alone started the operating system. A young Finnish programmer called Linus Torvalds was working on a new way to use a program called MINIX, a stripped-down version of an operating system called Unix that would change computing for ever.

Linus Torvalds

In 1991, he sent out a famous post to the Usenet group announcing his new operating system:

Hello everybody out there using minix - I'm doing a (free) operating system (just a hobby, won't be big and professional like gnu) for 386(486) AT clones. This has been brewing since April, and is starting to get ready. I'd like any feedback on things people like/dislike in minix, as my OS resembles it somewhat (same physical layout of the file-system (due to practical reasons) among other things).

The rest, as they say, is history. That post opened a new chapter in computing, one that led to the emergence of the Linux operating system in all its forms. It should be noted, however, that his original choice for his operating system was Freax (a mixture of free and Unix); the name Linux was actually devised by his collaborator Ari Lemmke. The first release of the software was proprietary, but it was quickly released under GPL.

SLACKWARE AND DEBIAN

In its early days, Linux was offered to users as a pair of floppy disks, one with the kernel, the other with a set of GNU tools. But the software wasn't intuitive and so an ecosystem of distributions (better known as distros) sprang up, which enabled users to adopt Linux more easily. Many of the early distros have fallen by the wayside, but two of the early ones still remain: Slackware and Debian. The latter is the precursor of many of today's distros and a whole load more have since emerged to fulfill users' needs (*see page 52*).

Hot Tip

Anyone interested in learning more about the history of Linux should read Glyn Moody's book *Rebel Code* – it is an excellent summary.

WHY LINUX?

That's a concise run-through of the history of Linux. Knowing the background doesn't actually help you to run the operating system, but it does help put in context why things are implemented the way they are. So what are the main reasons for selecting Linux?

There are many reasons users are turning to the operating system, and we run through some of them here. They're in no particular order; what may be the main reason for one person won't be for another.

LACK OF BLOATWARE

Remember when you first got your PC? You probably had to pick your way through an array of unwanted programs, certainly if you bought the machine from a large store. You would have had an antivirus product, possibly the magazine subscription offering, Zinio, and there would have been a package of various games. It is possible to remove these programs by using Uninstall, but it's a bit of a faff. By opting for Linux, you do away with such problems – there's no danger of being bombarded with reminders about trial periods ending, and certainly no pleas to pay for subscriptions to any services. With Linux, what you see is what you get.

THE VIRUS PROBLEM

Most people who have used Windows machines have experienced a virus attack at some point (and if you haven't been affected yourself, you may well have had to fix a machine for someone who has been). Viruses are so easy to create and can all too easily infect PCs: that link you shouldn't have clicked on; that CD you shouldn't have inserted; that program you shouldn't have run – all of these can bring their own problems.

Hot Tip

If you're constantly battling viruses, malware, or simply a slow computer that crashes a lot, Linux might be for you. It is the most stable operating system.

Linux is Virus Free

And don't you Apple users get smug and think that your machine is safe from attack: Macs get viruses too. In fact, if you really want to avoid any form of malware on your PC, Linux is the only way to go.

In theory, it's feasible for there to be a Linux virus but, as detailed earlier, there are many more eyes looking over Linux software. Vulnerabilities and weaknesses are spotted earlier and flaws are fixed more quickly.

CYBER CRIMINALS

Received wisdom is that the more people use an operating system, the more likely it is to have viruses. According to this theory, the reason that Windows is so vulnerable to attacks is because it's the most popular operating system – cyber criminals want to attack the system with the most users.

This implies that Linux is being ignored because there are so few users, but there's another overriding factor, which is to do with the way that Linux authenticates system changes.

Online Security

If you think about what happens with malware sent to a Windows machine, you can see why you may need tougher authentication rules. We've all heard the warnings about viruses and what not to do: don't open website links from unknown senders; don't load CDs of unknown provenance; keep your antivirus software up to date, and so on.

Linux Password Protection

When warnings about what not to do are ignored, the virus or the Trojan is able to interfere with the underlying operating system and cause all sorts of mayhem. It's not been unknown for a victim to have to install the operating system completely from scratch.

That can't happen with Linux, as you need an authentication password if you want to make a change to the underlying operating system. So, unless you have an especially smart virus that can not only muck up the innards of your computer, but also read your password, you're going to be in the clear.

LACK OF DRIVERS

If you want to attach any type of hardware to your computer – a printer, a scanner, anything along those lines – then you need to run a small program called a driver. This is not a problem when you first set up the device, as it will be included on the installation disk. The problems will start when you want to use another computer and have to start all over again. In many cases, you won't have the installation CD, and even if you do have it, you then have to worry about whether you're using the latest version of the driver. What generally happens is that you need to search through a manufacturer's website and look down a long list of drivers. This isn't always a straightforward task, as you have to have an exact match with the product and it's not always easy to find a list of drivers on manufacturer websites.

This is a rigmarole that you don't have to go through with Linux, as vast numbers of drivers are already included in the Linux kernel. Devices work out of the box, first time round.

Below: Drivers are much easier to handle on Linux machines.

Above: GIMP is an alternative to Photoshop.

Below: LibreOffice offers advanced document creation and data processing.

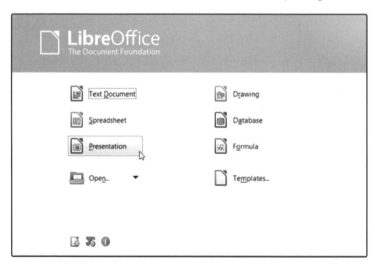

FREE SOFTWARE

As you've probably noticed, you don't have to worry about the cost of Linux software. You want to run word processing? Don't fork out for Microsoft Office, run LibreOffice instead. You want to manipulate images? Shove Photoshop to one side and choose GIMP. Want an email program? There's Thunderbird. In fact, you can pick most commercial software products and find there's a free Linux equivalent somewhere out there.

Linux and Creativity

Creative users are particularly fond of using Apple software and machines, and will be dismissive of any other software. However, Linux is perfectly capable of handling these types of demands. Besides GIMP, there are plenty of other products that can be deployed by creative professionals – DarkTable or RawStudio, for instance. And it doesn't stop with photo manipulation; for example, Laidout offers another way to do publishing; LibreOffice doesn't just do word processing but can offer more advanced features.

The Advantages of Open Source

Being free is not their only advantage (although that's not to be shrugged aside); it's the way that bugs are handled that's the real plus. Over the years, there have been plenty of bugs in Microsoft programs. It used to be an article of faith to wait for the second version as the company used to see its first efforts as a trial. Fixing these bugs takes time. That's not because Microsoft developers are less skilled but because the bureaucracy in a large company can slow everything down considerably.

That's not the case with open source products like Linux. As the name implies, everything is out in the open, with nothing hidden. That means that anyone can change the source code. In practice, this means little, because only skilled developers will be able to glean anything

significant from the code and be able to make alterations. But that doesn't matter: there are enough code experts out there who can do this and you can rest assured that there are going to be no malevolent developers (or if there are, they're going to be quickly found out). With Linux, there will be a bug tracker to report any flaws but, unlike Microsoft, you'll be able to see how the flaws are being fixed.

Hot Tip

Don't assume that there's no free equivalent for a program you use. Have a good look around and you're sure to find something that would fit.

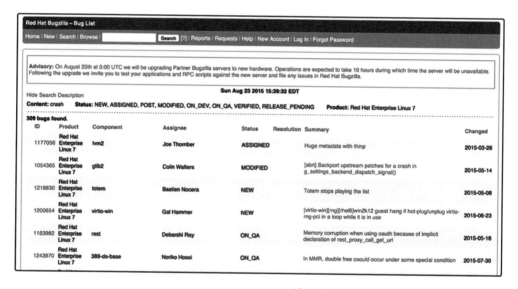

Above: Bug trackers are the open approach to fixing flaws.

NO BLUE SCREEN OF DEATH

We've all seen it: that dreadful blue screen telling us that something has gone wrong in Windows, with the inevitable message to restart your machine. It doesn't matter what version of Windows you have. XP? Vista? Windows 7? They're all susceptible to the dreaded screen. And yes, you get it with the new Windows 10 too.

The truth is, Windows does seem a bit more unstable than other operating systems – as Mac users are fond of pointing out – and there's an awful lot of restarting going on. It's become a standard joke for any sort of problem – turn it off and turn it on again. The truth is, that does work most of the time, but it's an inefficient way of dealing with problems.

Dealing with Updates

For a start, there are regular Windows updates to deal with. These are pretty essential for keeping the system fresh. Then you're probably updating the programs that run on your machine too. Every time you do that, you'll see a message about restarting – often when you're in the middle of something critical.

You can forget all of that with Linux. It just doesn't happen. There's no restart every time there's the slightest change to something on your machine. Whisper it quietly, but there are Linux machines out in the big world that have been running for years, nonstop, without once having been restarted.

POWERFUL SHELL

The way that Linux is structured is a central kernel (the core operating system, surrounded by Linux utilities) and then the shell (the part that the user deals with). For older Microsoft users, the Linux shell is a bit like returning to the days of DOS. You have to use a command-line interface and learn a whole truckload of commands. It's not intuitive like a GUI and there's a need to get your syntax exactly right; however, a shell can be more powerful than using a GUI, offering a level of control that you don't always get with fancier options. This, of course, is something we still see with Windows users; when there's something sophisticated that needs to be done, the GUI is shoved aside. Microsoft itself has recognized this with the introduction of PowerShell, a very powerful tool aimed at business users of Windows – a sign of how the Linux mentality has had an effect on more traditional companies.

Hot Tip

The shell, also known as the command line, was what used to scare people away from Linux. With a modern Linux desktop, there is no need to use the shell.

INTEROPERABILITY AND DUAL BOOTING

Linux plays well with other systems. It recognizes that there's a place for Windows and Mac OS X and will install alongside them, share files with them and generally be nice to them. This is very different from the Windows view that dual booting means choosing between Windows 7 and Vista.

There will be many Linux users for whom Windows is a must – maybe it's for a particular game, maybe it's for interoperability with business systems. In these circumstances, dual booting is not only an option, but almost essential.

Below: Linux works on a variety of hardware platforms, including on many sat-navs.

As a side-product of this, we should also note that Linux is pretty happy to run on a variety of hardware platforms. We've already seen how it's at the heart of a variety of devices from Tivo boxes to sat-nav kits, but it can also be used by any PC or laptop, including the popular Raspberry Pi machine. And in business, Linux can be deployed on any sort of chip architecture – from the Intel family to SPARC and IBM Power. More on this later.

THE RESTRICTIONS OF LINUX

It's worth pointing out that there's very little that Linux can't actually do: it's just that the experience is not going to be as smooth as it is with Windows or with Apple's iOS. You'll be able to do nearly everything with Linux that you do with these – it's just that there needs to be a bit of fiddling about and searching around. Don't let this put you off though, as that's half the fun of using Linux.

OPERABILITY

Linux is pretty interoperable with other software. But that's not to say that every Linux distro will run every piece of software that's ever been written. Even the most avid Linux user will admit that sometimes a particular distro will throw a wobbly when it tries to run an alien program.

As we saw with the City of Munich example on page 20, one of the elements that bedevils commercial implementations of Linux has been the inability of some Linux distros to work with Microsoft software which, given its dominance in the commercial world, is a pretty big black mark.

SOFTWARE AVAILABILITY

We've mentioned that there's free (or sometimes paid-for) software that can replace many of the commercial packages out there. That's true after a fashion, but what you're not getting is a like-for-like replacement. For example, GIMP is a great, free alternative to

Photoshop and can do about 99 per cent of all that the latter can do, but there are glaring gaps with GIMP. For example, it doesn't offer a CMYK option (commercial suicide for any software package that's looking to be used professionally). There's also a far richer ecosystem supporting Photoshop, offering a range of tools and add-ons that make life easier for the professional designer or art editor.

```
C:\Documents and Settings\Maxwell>cd\

C:\>dir\
 Volume in drive C has no label.
 Volume Serial Number is F8EF-1569

 Directory of C:\

15/08/2009  22:45    <DIR>          190dd2f38afade9e86be
25/02/2007  00:45    <DIR>          a4457c1213457f21d7ac4352db
05/02/2014  06:49    <DIR>          AdwCleaner
23/02/2008  10:09    <DIR>          All Users
10/08/2004  14:04                 0 AUTOEXEC.BAT
10/08/2004  14:04                 0 CONFIG.SYS
27/04/2013  06:49                 0 Cookies
08/12/2014  08:41    <DIR>          Db2729F8
01/06/2007  08:39    <DIR>          dell
19/06/2015  06:29    <DIR>          Documents and Settings
08/10/2006  14:57    <DIR>          drivers
11/12/2006  10:27    <DIR>          drvrtmp
12/08/2015  00:19                 0 drwtsn32.log
07/11/2007  09:00            17,734 eula.1028.txt
07/11/2007  09:00            17,734 eula.1031.txt
07/11/2007  09:00            10,134 eula.1033.txt
07/11/2007  09:00            17,734 eula.1036.txt
07/11/2007  09:00            17,734 eula.1040.txt
07/11/2007  09:00               118 eula.1041.txt
07/11/2007  09:00            17,734 eula.1042.txt
07/11/2007  09:00            17,734 eula.2052.txt
07/11/2007  09:00            17,734 eula.3082.txt
07/11/2007  09:00             1,110 globdata.ini
19/11/2014  21:04    <DIR>          i386
01/03/2007  10:21             4,128 INFCACHE.1
07/11/2007  09:00           562,688 install.exe
07/11/2007  09:00               843 install.ini
07/11/2007  09:03            76,304 install.res.1028.dll
07/11/2007  09:03            96,272 install.res.1031.dll
07/11/2007  09:03            91,152 install.res.1033.dll
07/11/2007  09:03            97,296 install.res.1036.dll
07/11/2007  09:03            95,248 install.res.1040.dll
07/11/2007  09:03            81,424 install.res.1041.dll
07/11/2007  09:03            79,888 install.res.1042.dll
07/11/2007  09:03            75,792 install.res.2052.dll
07/11/2007  09:03            96,272 install.res.3082.dll
11/11/2012  01:11    <DIR>          Kontiki
16/07/2008  15:23    <DIR>          logs
04/05/2014  10:35           262,144 NTUser.dat
15/08/2015  19:55    <DIR>          Program Files
20/09/2014  23:22    <DIR>          Python34
02/08/2014  12:18    <DIR>          temp
07/11/2007  09:00             5,686 vcredist.bmp
07/11/2007  09:09         1,442,522 VC_RED.cab
07/11/2007  09:12           232,960 VC_RED.MSI
16/08/2015  07:43    <DIR>          WINDOWS
              30 File(s)      3,436,119 bytes
              16 Dir(s)  12,223,504,384 bytes free
```

And it's not just Photoshop. There's any number of Windows or Mac programs that offer a far more sophisticated user experience. There are plenty of substitutes for the home user or the enthusiastic amateur, but the hardcore professional needs much more.

LACK OF GUI

Anyone who uses Windows machines or Macs has an easy-to-use Graphical User Interface (GUI) to help them negotiate the operating system. The GUI has been part of Apple since for ever but (this is hard to think now) Windows has only been using a GUI since the early 1990s. Anyone who was using Microsoft before that would have had to work with DOS and that meant learning a host of DOS commands. Intuitive it was not.

That's not to say that you can't run a GUI on Linux, it's just that they're not integrated with the operating system in the same way that Windows is with Microsoft machines. But various distros have their GUI options – Mint has an option called Cinnamon, for example, and there are plenty of others to work with.

RUNNING GAMES

If you're a hardcore gamer, you're going to want to stick to Windows. All game vendors will have to support Microsoft (even Macs play second fiddle when it comes to games). Linux is just not on the map when it comes to gaming software.

Below: Alienware laptops running Windows are very popular with gamers.

PCS WITH PRE-INSTALLED LINUX

If you're buying a computer from the likes of PC World or an online retailer such as Dabs, it's going to come with Windows pre-installed (unless you're buying a Mac, which will come with iOS pre-installed). And what if you want to buy a machine with Linux on it? Well, there's the rub: there are a few places that will do it, but you'll have to search around.

No major manufacturer has gone down that route since Dell launched a range of Linux desktop machines ... and discontinued them a few months later. The reason for this is pure economics: there's much more demand for Windows machines and, as such, the mass market drives the economies of scale needed to bring the price down. You can also throw in the bloatware programs mentioned earlier. Yes, they're a pain, but their vendors pay to be included and they do help to bring the price down even more.

And if companies did offer Linux machines, what would they offer? Debian? Ubuntu? Mint? Fedora? You just know that any decision made would immediately raise the hackles of a legion of fans for an alternative system.

Hot Tip
If you're looking to run a home server, then you do have the option of pre-installed Linux. Dell and a few smaller vendors offer it.

WATCH VIDEOS

We're all used to watching video content on our computer screens. The TV is less in favour as a way of getting our fix and we're using PCs, tablets and smartphones more and more.

It isn't quite true that Linux won't let you watch videos: there are workarounds that can be employed to watch videos, but they're not straightforward. What most people want to do is switch on the device, click on a website and watch – this is something that's not always immediately possible with Linux, but don't worry, there are still options available.

Have a look around for tools out there that are capable of doing this; the best known is Banshee, which allows users to watch videos or listen to music. It's renowned for being exceptionally fast, as well as being interoperable with all distros (it even works with iPods). It's included as standard with some distros, such as OpenSUSE.

Below: The ability to watch videos on a Linux computer is more complex than on Windows or iOS, but it can definitely be achieved.

Hot Tip

There are plenty of media players for Linux. Miro doesn't only let you watch videos, it also provides access to a range of video content too. Established player VideoLAN has a Linux option for its VLC player. MPlayer (and its associated front-end SMPlayer), MPV, Kaffeine, Gnome Videos and Tomahawk are all other options to try as well.

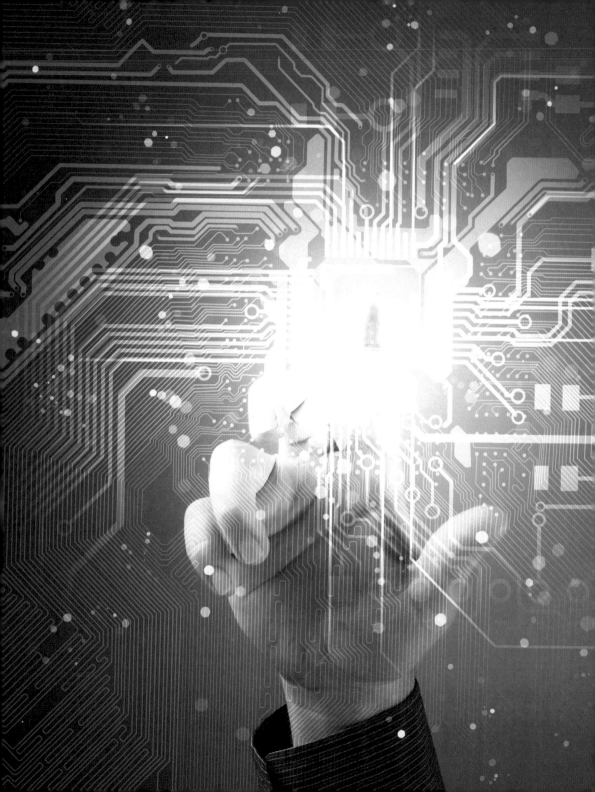

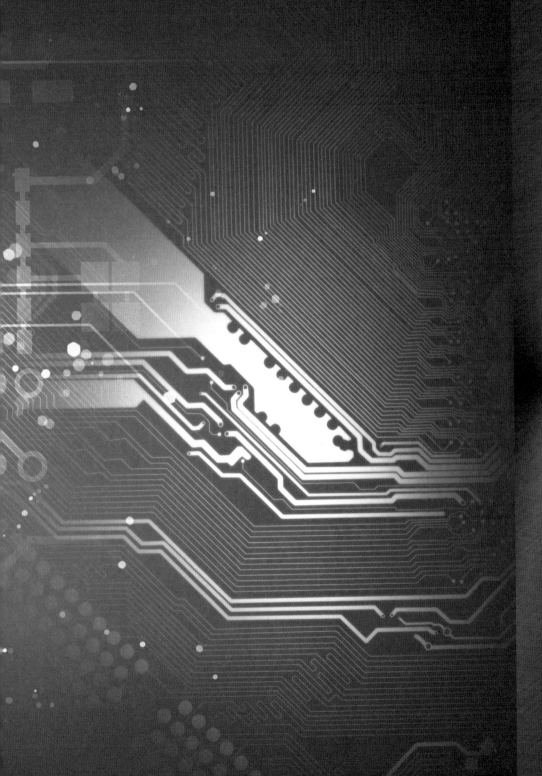

THE LINUX ECOSYSTEM

THE KERNEL AND THE SHELL

Every concept in computing has a handful of key components, and Linux has two: the kernel and the shell. The kernel is the central aspect of the operating system – the core lump of code without which it wouldn't be Linux.

THE KERNEL

The Linux kernel is unusual among operating system core code in that it's freely available and you can download and build it yourself. In the early 1990s, the source code fitted on a handful of floppy disks. At the time of writing, the most recent version available is release 4.1.3, which

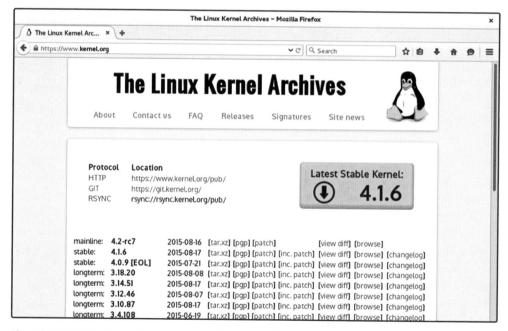

Above: Developers around the world have contributed to The Linux Kernel Archives to improve the performance of Linux.

```
51    char *EXP_COM[] = {"-?","-L?",
52    char *RV_TIME[] = {"0 seconds",

53
54
55    int summary(void *barg,void *arg)
56    {
57            char *str = (char *)arg;
58            st_board *board = (st_board
59            int ret = 0;
60
              char *ptr_shuttercounter =
```

Above: An example of the source code for an operating system.

is a download of about 80MB in size. As soon as Linux started to become popular, people around the world started to produce more and more features. Each release of the kernel absorbed more and more of these options, but of course, the average user didn't want or need most of them. Back in the days where memory and disk space were scarce, if your computer had an Ethernet adaptor, you didn't want to use RAM to host the code for a Token Ring card. Similarly, if your network used IP addressing, you wanted to save the space that would have been occupied by the code that supported IPX or DECnet. The solution was easy: the kernel source code gave you an interactive menu system that let you pick the bits you wanted before building the code.

EVERYTHING CHANGES BUT YOU

And you know what? You can still use precisely the same interface to do the same thing. To be fair, it's rather more complicated than it was 20 years ago, but that's only because there are so many more new technologies and concepts supported in today's Linux kernel than there were back in the day.

Below: Building a kernel isn't a quick process, but it is relatively simple.

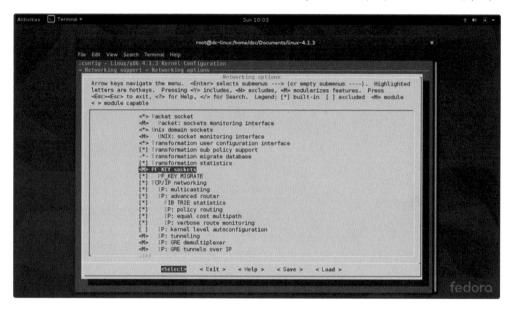

Building a kernel is a really simple process of following an idiot-proof guide, making sure you have a couple of simple prerequisites on your system, running the configuration program and then telling it to build. The actual build isn't the most complicated bit of running up your own kernel – it's understanding what's meant by the plethora of options you're presented with in the menu-based configuration tool. Oh, and it's not something you just run off in a minute or two: I just ran a kernel build on my Acer laptop based on the default options and it took about an hour and 40 minutes.

THE ESSENTIAL DEVELOPMENT

The fundamentals of the kernel are largely the same today as they were at launch. The most important exception is the Loadable Kernel Module, or LKM. You'll probably be familiar with Windows computers that prompt you, when you connect a new gadget, to install a driver – the lump of code that allows the kernel to interface to that new device. In the very early days of

Below: The Loadable Kernel Modules, or LKMs, that are in use can be seen here.

```
                                   dsc@linuxpc-local:~                                    ✕

 File   Edit   View   Search   Terminal   Help
auth_rpcgss              65536   1 nfsd
nfs_acl                  16384   1 nfsd
lockd                    94208   1 nfsd
grace                    16384   2 nfsd,lockd
sunrpc                  311296   7 nfsd,auth_rpcgss,lockd,nfs_acl
i915                   1077248   7
i2c_algo_bit             16384   1 i915
rtsx_pci_sdmmc           24576   0
drm_kms_helper          118784   1 i915
8021q                    32768   0
drm                     331776   8 i915,drm_kms_helper
garp                     16384   1 8021q
stp                      16384   2 garp,bridge
llc                      16384   3 stp,garp,bridge
mrp                      20480   1 8021q
r8169                    86016   0
rtsx_pci                 53248   2 rtsx_pci_ms,rtsx_pci_sdmmc
mii                      16384   1 r8169
mfd_core                 16384   2 lpc_ich,rtsx_pci
sdhci_acpi               16384   0
sdhci                    45056   1 sdhci_acpi
mmc_core                126976   3 sdhci,sdhci_acpi,rtsx_pci_sdmmc
video                    24576   2 i915,acer_wmi
[dsc@linuxpc-local ~]$
```

Linux, assuming someone had written the appropriate piece of code, you'd have had to download the kernel source code, drop in the custom code, compile a new kernel and restart the computer. The introduction of the LKM enabled users to drop in the code 'module' and tell the kernel to read it in on the fly, without the need to rebuild from scratch or reboot the machine.

SHELLING OUT

So we've interfaced to the hardware using the kernel, and we can now run programs on our Linux machine. That's fine, but how do we actually configure the system and navigate around it? How do we copy files, check disk space, set up the wireless network or configure the system so it can print?

Left: Many old PCs, such as this one from the 1980s, would only be capable of displaying a text-based interface, called a shell.

Text-based Interface

The answer today is that we wave our mice around and click on things. But that's not the traditional way with Unix and Linux. And anyway, in the early days, PC technology was very primitive and a GUI wasn't even an option – many PCs just didn't have graphics cards or screens capable of displaying anything more than a basic text-based interface into which you typed commands. And that interface was – and is – called a shell.

Hot Tip

As you'll see, the shells all have their own variations on how you do things. Play with them all and pick your favourite.

Intriguingly, though, unlike some operating systems where you have Hobson's choice regarding shells, there are actually loads of different shells for the Linux platform (see page 68).

WHAT DOES THE SHELL DO?

One of the things to bear in mind with the shell is that it doesn't actually know how to execute very many commands. The commands you execute in Linux – for example ls to list the files in a directory, or df to check the disk space usage on your computer – are actually separate programs. The shell is merely giving you a mechanism to say, for instance, 'Run program ls' when you want to see the files on the disk. The shell tells the kernel to open the program file you've selected; the program hooks directly into the kernel in order to do its work. Think of a Linux command as a program – it's a lump of code that does some processing based on what you tell it.

In this example, we'll run ls to list the contents of the current directory:

```
[dsc@localhost ~]$ ls
Desktop   Documents   Downloads   Music   Pictures   Public
Templates   Videos
```

... and here, we'll use df to show the disk space usage:

```
[dsc@localhost ~]$ df
Filesystem          1K-blocks       Used  Available  Use%  Mounted on
devtmpfs             4037856           0    4037856    0%  /dev
tmpfs                4048792         564    4048228    1%  /dev/shm
tmpfs                4048792        1592    4047200    1%  /run
tmpfs                4048792           0    4048792    0%  /sys/fs/cgroup
/dev/mapper/fedora-root   51475068  7585796   41251448   16%  /
tmpfs                4048792         140    4048652    1%  /tmp
/dev/sda6             487652      119058     338898   26%  /boot
/dev/sda2             303104       58800     244304   20%  /boot/efi
/dev/mapper/fedora-home  399626304   103852  379199536    1%  /home
tmpfs                809760           8     809752    1%  /run/user/42
tmpfs                809760          20     809740    1%  /run/user/1000
```

The writers of shells have historically been in competition to make their offering more attractive than the others, which means that they try to make life as easy as possible for the user. We'll look at differences later, but you'll find that all of them have lots in common. For instance, you can:

- Run backwards and forwards through your command history using the cursor keys on your keyboard.

- List the commands you've recently executed.

- Create aliases as shorthand for commonly used commands.

- Set a search path so that when you type a command, it'll search in different places to find the program it needs.

- Set most shells to colour-code the output of commands like `ls` based on the file type.

- Limit what you can run, to ensure nothing runs away with the system resources.

- Tell the shell to run a program in the background – detach it from the shell so you can even kill off the shell without killing the program.

The Prompt

And in the command examples we just gave, you may have noticed the bit on the line where we've typed the command – the prompt:

```
[dsc@localhost ~]$
```

This is something all shells can do – provide you with a prompt that tells you useful stuff. In this case it's telling us:

- `dsc@localhost`: We're logged in as user dsc on a machine called localhost.

- `~`: We're currently working in the home directory of the current user (~ is shorthand for 'home directory' in Linux).

- `$`: We're running as a normal user (it'd be # if we were the privileged 'root' user).

We'll come back later to a comparison of the popular shells you're likely to come across in an average Linux distribution (see page 68). Some will install by default and others are options that you can turn on very easily.

> ## Hot Tip
> Get used to the meanings of the shell prompt – they include useful information like whether you're running as a normal user or the 'root' user, or what directory you're working in.

WHAT IS A DISTRO?

We've already seen that the kernel enables us to run programs, and the shell lets us actually tell it to do so – but what about the programs themselves? Where do they come from? This is where the distros come in. They're bundles that bring together all the items you need to take your combination of the Linux kernel and the shell and make it useful.

COMMANDS

At the basic level, we have the commands that let us manage the Linux computer. So it's commands like ls and df that we saw in the examples given earlier, but in fact there are many hundreds of these that do an enormous amount. So there's gzip for compressing files, mount to connect local and remote disk storage, ping to check if a remote computer is responding ... the list goes on far longer than we can accommodate here.

CODE LIBRARIES

All operating systems have libraries – collections of common functions that programmers can use when writing their code. The idea's a simple one: where there are functions that loads of programmers use all the time, why not write them once, include them as part of the operating system, and let the programmers call them from their code? The really common functions are things like string manipulation (reversing strings, counting string lengths and so on) or trigonometric functions. There's a boatload of other, far more complicated stuff in the average Linux distro.

```
root@linuxpc-local:~                                                        ✕

File  Edit  View  Search  Terminal  Help
STRSTR(3)                    Linux Programmer's Manual                STRSTR(3)

NAME
        strstr, strcasestr - locate a substring

SYNOPSIS
        #include <string.h>

        char *strstr(const char *haystack, const char *needle);

        #define _GNU_SOURCE             /* See feature_test_macros(7) */

        #include <string.h>

        char *strcasestr(const char *haystack, const char *needle);

DESCRIPTION
        The  strstr() function finds the first occurrence of the substring nee-
        dle in the string haystack.  The terminating null bytes ('\0') are  not
        compared.
```

Above: The Linux Programmer's Manual showing the Library Function.

PACKAGE MANAGER

In the old days, distros came on CDs and DVDs. These days, you can still download an entire distro, but with modern, high-speed internet connectivity, it's equally common to start with a very small 'get started' installer image and then for the installer to download just the bits it needs.

To do this, the distro manufacturers have produced package managers – applications that bundle all the key components of a program into a single package, which you can then download and extract. The contents are pulled out of the package and placed in various

Above: This is Yumex, a graphical package manager for Fedora.

> # Hot Tip
>
> **Get to know your package manager – it's great to be able to interrogate your Linux system easily to see what's installed, and what version it is.**

appropriate locations around your computer's disk. The package manager also knows about any dependencies that the software in one package has on other items, so if you try to install something that depends on a piece of software you don't have, it will tell you and offer to download and install it for you.

A Big Win for Linux

To give you an idea of what a huge benefit the package manager offers, let's take the MySQL database package as an example. On my test PC, I compared the time taken to compile and install MySQL from scratch with the time taken to install it from the prepackaged version that comes with the Fedora distro. With the self-compile option, it took an hour to obtain the right prerequisites, compile the software, install the programs, tweak the configuration files and fire up the server. Installation using the prebuilt package took about three minutes, including firing up the server once installed. The self-build took about 40 minutes for the compilation alone – and that's without installing the prerequisite programs, downloading and unzipping the archive, etc. Using the package manager, it took three minutes to go from nothing to a running MySQL server. The package manager is one of Linux distros' big wins.

DOCUMENTATION

Documentation is absolutely key to any computer system, and Linux has it in spades. The basic documentation used by Unix-style operating systems since the year dot has been the man (manual) page. The man command shows text-based documentation, with basic formatting, through which you can page forward and back. For instance, the man page for the df command is shown below.

The man library is still core to Linux, and core to looking up how the various commands you type work. When it comes to application documentation it's far more common either to have this in PDF form, in a browser-readable form on the machine, or on the Web.

Hot Tip

Manual pages look basic, but they're the core documentation of Linux commands. Everything you need to know about commands will be in there, often with examples of how to use them.

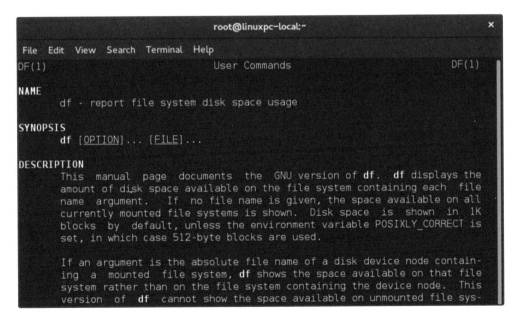

Above: The manual or man page for the df command.

APPLICATIONS

Open source software has the benefit of enabling you to download the source code and compile it yourself. But unless you want to customize the code, why would you want to? To compile a typical open source application, you need to install a compiler and often a collection of other tools, which is a chore – particularly if you're a nonexpert and you come across errors that you don't understand.

Above: The Ubuntu Software Centre is an application store for Linux.

Distros therefore include collections of common applications that the producers have taken the time to compile, build and bundle into packages that can be installed simply and quickly using the package manager approach we discussed earlier. This collection of applications can only be described as enormous, regardless of which distro you're using; it ranges from trivial games, through useful system utilities, to high-performance email and database software.

How does an application differ from the concept of a command that we mentioned earlier? In reality, there's a grey area between the two. The differentiation I make is that a command is something that you run once to produce one answer (a list of programs running on the machine using ps, for instance), while an application is anything more complicated than that.

GUIS

Linux in its basic form is a text-based operating system – you have a command line to type things into, and it tells you things by writing text on the screen. The other core software component distros include, then, is the desktop environment – a graphical desktop that lets you use a mouse to run graphical applications, over many screens if you wish, just like you're used to on every other operating system.

Below: The default Graphical User Interface, or GUI, for Fedora is shown here.

Distro producers generally offer you more than one desktop environment; really, they're just applications like any other, but they happen to be aimed at providing a graphical interface to Linux. Most distros have a default desktop environment that gets installed if you do a Next ➜ Next ➜ Next setup, but you'll usually have the option to switch if you don't like their choice for any reason (switching from the standard Fedora desktop to KDE on our test machine took a 345MB download and a couple of commands, for instance).

STANDARD CONFIGURATION

The programs in a Linux distro come from a wide range of different developers. As we've said, the producers of the distro take the applications, configure and compile them, and include them as packages in the distro. But they don't just download the source code of each application and compile it: they plan a system-wide directory structure and arrange all of the applications so that configuration files are all stored in a single, comprehensive directory structure. The default location for things like configuration files and executable programs differs from application to application, so the distro producers go to great pains to organize everything and change the locations from the app developers' defaults to directories that are common across everything they include in the distro.

This is particularly important when apps are interdependent. For example, it's common to run database-backed websites on Linux – the popular approach is to combine the Apache web server, the PHP development language and the MySQL database. Distros are built so that each of these is already set up to work immediately with the others, with no need for further tweaking, because they're built to a common configuration and directory layout. This approach saves vast amounts of time, so a bit of gratitude to the distro makers is in order.

THE DISTRO IS THE BUNDLE

A Linux distro is more than the sum of its parts. In its basic form, it brings together a kernel, a collection of commands and a set of applications, and wraps an installer program around them. But the real value of a distro is the tremendous coherence between all of the components – the standardized directory structure and the fact that the packages are compatible with each other, having been built based on a set of standards. Add in the package manager that lets you add in and drop out elements at will and the distro's value is clear.

Hot Tip

When you've explored a few applications, you'll start to find your way around the common places for configuration files without really thinking about it.

THE PROS AND CONS OF THE MAIN VENDORS

Although it's an open source concept, there are actually several very popular commercial Linux offerings. Why would you want to pay for something that you can download for free? Simple: stability and support.

PAY FOR PEACE OF MIND

It can't be denied that the free Linux distributions are, generally, well tested and incredibly stable – but there's no guarantee of this. The author once broke part of his network simply

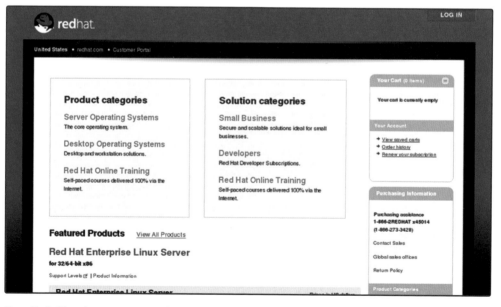

Above: The Red Hat online store is one option if you'd prefer to pay for a distro that is likely to be more stable than other open source distros.

by setting the IP address of a Linux server using its standard configuration interface; it turned out there was a bug in the GUI that caused it to set addresses incorrectly with spectacularly crashy results. The commercial vendors are able to apply more rigorous testing to the distributions they offer.

EXTRAS INCLUDED

At this point, it's important to remember that a Linux distro – commercial or otherwise – comprises not only the kernel and core Linux executables but also the fleet of included apps. The commercial vendors have their own repositories of applications, from which their paid-for Linux offerings download updates to the (often complicated) suites of applications that form part of the distro. So you'll generally find that new versions of applications – particularly complex ones – come out more frequently in the free Linux distros than they do in the commercial ones, as the commercial providers prefer fewer releases with more testing per release.

Hot Tip

Decide whether you want a distro that always has new versions or one that sticks with older, more stable ones. If it's a home machine, we go for the ones that use new stuff.

SUSE

SUSE (originally SuSE) is an abbreviation of Software und System-Entwicklung, or 'Software and System Development' when translated from German. The SUSE distribution has been regarded by many as what you would expect of German design – solid and stable without shouting about itself. Having established itself as a standalone entity in the Linux market, the company was acquired by Novell in 2003–4 and, through various other mergers and acquisitions, is now a part of Micro Focus group.

SUSE has made a big deal of its industry partnerships over the years, and it still trumpets its 'special' relationships with Microsoft, SAP and VMware. If you're an enterprise using SAP, then it's fair to say SUSE would be a no-brainer choice for platform. On the VMware front: does the preference for SUSE mean other Linuxes won't work? Of course not, but you'd be silly to disregard any kind of vendor tie-up that might imply more robust interoperability testing, or that both parties' developers have sat in darkened rooms discussing how to eke more out of each other's platforms.

SUSE still has an open source offering, of course, called openSUSE.

RED HAT

Red Hat is a huge name in commercial Linux implementations. Founded in 1993, the company became hugely well known by the late 1990s, because it made Linux so much easier than before. The Red Hat Package Manager (RPM) suddenly made application installation and update far easier than before (you'll recall that we discussed the benefits of package managers earlier), and the company's online subscription and upgrade mechanism allowed the user to update their installation with far more confidence than doing it by hand.

Red Hat Enterprise Linux, or RHEL as it's generally known, is popular because of its longevity. Because Red Hat did it first, application developers have had a much longer timescale over which they've been able to tune their code to work fastest and most reliably with RHEL. It's also very easy to find formal training and certification programmes for RHEL.

Finally, the longevity of the Red Hat family brings with it a vast community of people using Fedora and CentOS (the open source offerings of the family). So if you're one of those people and you're looking to move to a general purpose, commercially supported Linux, then Red Hat will be the easiest one to learn thanks to the family resemblance.

Hot Tip
RHEL is pretty much the daddy of commercial Linux distros, and is the name everyone knows. Don't let that put you off the others though – they have their benefits too.

Below: The Red Hat headquarters in Raleigh, North Carolina.

UBUNTU

Ubuntu varies the model slightly because there isn't a commercial version and an open source version as such. Ubuntu is a free offering, but its development is supported by Canonical – a company that makes its real money from selling a portfolio of services and supports development of the Ubuntu Linux distro with that income.

Since there's no programme of commercial releases, the Ubuntu project instead selects every fourth version to be regarded as a highly supported release, with new versions every sixth months or so. This means you get long-term support (or 'LTS') offerings every couple of years.

Although the likes of Red Hat and SUSE have the server market largely cornered, this doesn't mean Ubuntu's not worth considering. It has a reputation for being highly usable, and so is

Below: Canonical offer support for the distro Ubuntu with their official guides.

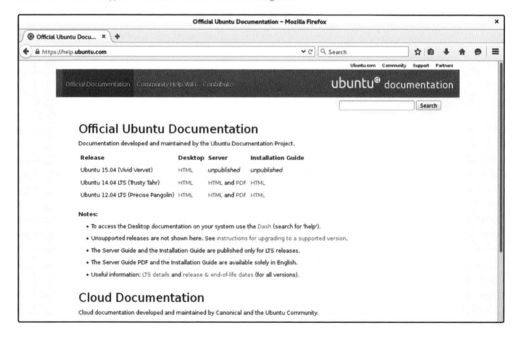

attractive if you're considering running Linux on nontechies' desktops – in fact, some PC vendors ship it as an alternative to Windows. It's also seeing popularity in non-PC devices – mobiles and tablets, for instance.

ORACLE

Oracle Linux isn't really a Linux distro all of its own, but is in fact derived from Red Hat Enterprise Linux (though Oracle has produced its own so-called 'Unbreakable Enterprise Kernel' that claims to be both superior to and compatible with the Red Hat offering). It's no surprise that Oracle is determined to take over the world and to entice RHEL customers to its own offering. To be fair, it's not an unattractive offering, since Oracle Linux is free to download and distribute, and you can choose to have a paid-for support option.

Below: Oracle Linux is free but has an optional support option, for a fee.

If you're looking for a general, mainstream Linux, then Oracle Linux isn't the obvious choice. You would, however, consider it if you have a heavy leaning towards Oracle's application products, since over time there will inevitably be performance benefits in having applications running on their vendor's home-produced operating system. Incidentally, don't forget that this doesn't just mean the commercial Oracle apps – they also own the likes of the MySQL database application, which started life in the open source world.

NOTABLE OTHERS

The Linux providers we've mentioned are few, but they cover the vast majority of Linux installations worldwide. It is, however, worth giving a quick mention to a handful of others.

AMI

First, Amazon's Linux AMI. As you might guess, this is a Linux flavour that was produced and is maintained by Amazon. If you're going to use Linux Amazon's EC2 cloud server platform, this is unsurprisingly an attractive option, as you can be sure of compatibility and performance.

Debian

Next, we have Debian Linux. In truth, it's no longer a big deal in its own right. In fact, there's a very close relationship between Debian and Ubuntu, but it's the latter that is seeing popularity – primarily because of the development and support umbrella provided by Canonical. So Debian's far from dead, but people do tend to lean towards Ubuntu.

Android

Finally, let's mention an operating system you might not have been expecting to read about: Android. It's been estimated that Android runs on more devices worldwide than any other operating system, and it's easy to forget that it's actually based on the Linux kernel. Of course, Android isn't a Linux distro in the sense discussed earlier; it's a fairly tight set of components designed for a specific purpose. A standard Linux distribution comes with a set of developer tools onboard but to write apps for Android you run a developer tool on a separate PC. Nonetheless, don't forget that Android is actually Linux under the hood.

SO WHICH DO I GO FOR?

There's no right answer, but the guidance is pretty simple: if you have a specific requirement that's met by one of the commercial offerings (Oracle apps, for example), then veer towards that offering. If you're looking for a hybrid of commercially supported and DIY, then the Ubuntu model is probably for you. If you want to take advantage of support for non-Intel processors, then have a Google for the CPU you need to support (IBM's Power range is an option for SUSE, for example). And if you're a generalist, then it's hard not to go for Red Hat.

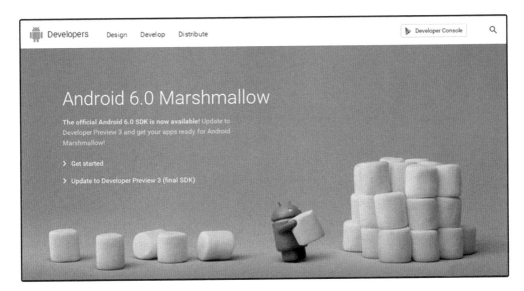

Above: Android is an increasingly popular operating system.

SHELLS – KEEPING IT IN THE FAMILY

As we've already mentioned, the shell is what you type commands into in order to get your Linux machine to do your bidding. And as with most things in Linux, you have a number of options when it comes to which shell to use. Although there are several options, there were originally two separate families.

THE BOURNE SHELL FAMILY

The Bourne shell – usually implemented by an executable program called sh – was first developed by Stephen Bourne at Bell Labs. Like the other shells one finds in Linux implementations, it pre-dates the Linux kernel by many years – it first appeared in the late 1970s as part of Bell Labs' Unix implementation. The Bourne shell is known as sh – and this is the name of the executable program on a Linux machine.

THE C SHELL FAMILY

While Bell Labs was producing its Unix implementation, the University of California in Berkeley was producing its own Unix-like flavour, called the Berkeley Software Distribution, or BSD. Graduate student Bill Joy was the core creator, and the C shell also appeared in the late 1970s. The C shell is known as – and its executable is called – csh.

THE DERIVATIVES

Unsurprisingly, shells have come a long way since the late 1970s – it would be a shock if nothing had changed in 30-odd years, after all. There has been a boatload of different derivatives, which fall into two camps: direct descendants and hybrids.

TCSH - SON OF CSH

Tcsh, a product of Ken Greer at Carnegie Mellon University, is about the purest derivative of any of the more modern Unix/Linux shells. The author merged his various developments into the C shell in the early 1980s, so there's no real overlap with the sh family. The main additions that tcsh brings when compared to csh is the introduction of filename auto-completion (so if

Below: The tcsh shell is not installed by default. Here it is being installed.

```
                           root@linuxpc-local:~                              ×

File  Edit  View  Search  Terminal  Help
[root@linuxpc-local ~]# dnf install tcsh
Last metadata expiration check performed 0:24:37 ago on Mon Aug 17 20:16:43 2015.
Dependencies resolved.
================================================================================
 Package          Arch            Version              Repository        Size
================================================================================
Installing:
 tcsh             x86_64          6.18.01-13.fc22         fedora          344 k

Transaction Summary
================================================================================
Install  1 Package

Total download size: 344 k
Installed size: 662 k
Is this ok [y/N]: y
Downloading Packages:
tcsh-6.18.01-13.fc22.x86_64.rpm            593 kB/s | 344 kB     .00:00
--------------------------------------------------------------------------------
Total                                      208 kB/s | 344 kB     00:01
Running transaction check
Transaction check succeeded.
Running transaction test
Transaction test succeeded.
Running transaction
  Installing  : tcsh-6.18.01-13.fc22.x86_64                            1/1
  Verifying   : tcsh-6.18.01-13.fc22.x86_64                            1/1

Installed:
  tcsh.x86_64 6.18.01-13.fc22

Complete!
[root@linuxpc-local ~]#
```

you hit the appropriate key and there's only one possible way for it to guess what you mean, it'll do so) and a load of mechanisms for referring back to historical commands.

THE HYBRIDS

Bash, or the 'Bourne Again Shell', was developed as an open source alternative to the Bourne shell. It has long been one of the standard shells for Linux, and if you install Linux without changing any of the options, you're likely to end up with this as your default. Although seemingly named after (and including, largely unchanged, the functionality of) sh, it incorporates features of csh and ksh as well. Extras on top of basic sh functionality are command completion (hit the right key and if there's only one possible option for the half-typed command, it'll finish it for you), some useful shorthands for file redirection, and some nice scripting features such as advanced array structures. We'll come back to scripting later. Ksh, or the 'Korn shell', is named after its author David Korn. Although heavily sh-like, again there are features shared with csh, such as command aliasing and command history.

THE POSIX SHELL STANDARD

Sh, csh, tcsh, bash and ksh are the five shells you'll come across pretty well all of the time – and as we've seen, they're all slightly different. Yet there is actually a standard that defines the core requirements for a Unix-style shell, which is part of the IEEE 1003 family of specifications. So if there's a standard, why are there so many shells? Simple: the functionality that satisfies the POSIX specification is merely a subset of what each of these shells offers. Developers use POSIX as a minimum starting point and build on it in the hope of persuading users to like their flavour rather than someone else's.

Oh, and in case you're wondering, the POSIX spec was based on the 1988 version of ksh.

FUNKY SHELLS – AN HONOURABLE MENTION

The shells we've mentioned are the ones you're going to come across. There are, however, a few special-purpose shells for those of an adventurous disposition. For example:

- **Fish**: the 'friendly interactive shell', which is designed to be friendlier than traditional shells. It has neither sh nor csh in its heritage.

- **Scsh**: a shell that's based on the Scheme programming language.

- **Wish**: a shell that lets you use GUI components.

These shells have very little in common other than the fact that you're unlikely ever to use them.

COMPARISONS – STARTING AND STOPPING

Now we know a little bit about the various shells on our Linux machines, let's look at some of the practical differences. Although you can use any of the shells in its raw form, each one of them gives you the ability to write configuration files that set it up the way you want it: to set the prompt you get on the command line, for example, or to define aliases for commands you use a lot.

Unhelpfully, different shells use different start-up files. Let's compare bash and tcsh; we'll look at what configuration files they look for first, and will then explain what's actually done.

When you log in with bash, it first checks for a system-wide configuration file:

```
/etc/profile
```

Before we go further, it's important to note that nothing breaks if any of these start-up files doesn't exist. If it's there, the shell will process it; if it's not, it won't not worry and will carry on to the next file it hopes to see.

Home Directory

Every user ID on a Linux machine has a default home directory. If you're a normal user, this will be a private directory, and so you can use a local config file in your home directory to specify any customizations you want. In the case of bash it'll look for three alternative files in your home directory:

```
.bash_profile
.bash_login
.profile
```

It'll look for the files in this order and will process only the first it comes across. The last of the three, .profile, is a kickback to the old sh days – it was the default name for the personal config file. Note that if you use both sh and ksh (if you feel so inclined), then it's common to add an entry to .bash_profile that references .profile, then to put your bash-only commands in .bash_profile and your sh-compatible commands in .profile. Sh will process just the latter, and bash will process both.

Here goes with an example. We'll start with a user that has a .bash_profile and a .profile. The former sets the command prompt to start with bash_profile, and the latter with profile. We'd expect the prompt to mention bash_profile, and indeed it does:

```
Davids-MacBook-Pro:~ davidcartwright$ ssh dsc@192.168.1.186
dsc@192.168.1.186's password:
```

```
Last login: Mon Jul 27 21:02:13 2015
bash_profile@21:02:42:~$
```

Now we'll delete the `.bash_profile` and we'd expect it to pick up `.profile`, and sure enough, it does:

```
Davids-MacBook-Pro:~ davidcartwright$ ssh dsc@192.168.1.186
dsc@192.168.1.186's password:
Last login: Mon Jul 27 21:02:42 2015 from 192.168.1.156
profile@21:02:54:~$
```

Below: The etc profile for bash.

```
root@linuxpc-local:~                              ✕

File  Edit  View  Search  Terminal  Help
# /etc/profile

# System wide environment and startup programs, for login setup
# Functions and aliases go in /etc/bashrc

# It's NOT a good idea to change this file unless you know what you
# are doing. It's much better to create a custom.sh shell script in
# /etc/profile.d/ to make custom changes to your environment, as this
# will prevent the need for merging in future updates.

pathmunge () {
    case ":${PATH}:" in
        *:"$1":*)
            ;;
        *)
            if [ "$2" = "after" ] ; then
                PATH=$PATH:$1
            else
                PATH=$1:$PATH
            fi
    esac
}

if [ -x /usr/bin/id ]; then
```

Now on to the tcsh shell, which takes a different approach – in fact, it sometimes feels like it wants to run every config file in the known universe. The system-wide start-up files are:

```
/etc/csh.cshrc
/etc/csh.login
```

Then we have a selection of files that live in your home directory:

```
.tcshrc
.cshrc
.login
```

Below: The system-wide start-up files for the tcsh shell.

```
Open ▾  ⊓                    csh.cshrc [Read–Only]                    Save  ≡  ✕
                                   /etc
# /etc/cshrc
#
# csh configuration for all shell invocations.

# By default, we want this to get set.
# Even for non-interactive, non-login shells.
# Current threshold for system reserved uid/gids is 200
# You could check uidgid reservation validity in
# /usr/share/doc/setup-*/uidgid file
if ($uid > 199 && "`id -gn`" == "`id -un`") then
    umask 002
else
    umask 022
endif

if ($?prompt) then
  if ($?tcsh) then
    set promptchars='$#'
    set prompt='[%n@%m %c]%# '
    # make completion work better by default
    set autolist
  else
    set prompt=\[$user@`hostname -s`\]\$\
  endif
endif

if ( $?tcsh ) then
        bindkey "^[[3~" delete-char
endif

bindkey "^R" i-search-back
set echo style = both
```

In a similar way that we mentioned about bash, csh will only run .cshrc if it doesn't find .tcshrc, so you can reference one from the other if you have a burning desire to swap between shells. Note that there's a variety of other stuff tcsh will read by default, but we won't go there as the ones we've mentioned are the important ones.

Tcsh Shell

Here's a tcsh shell example. Let's start with a tcsh user that has both a .tcshrc and a .cshrc file. The .tcshrc sets the command prompt so it starts with the string tcshrc, and .cshrc sets it to start with cshrc; we're connecting to our Fedora box using SSH from a Mac:

```
Davids-MacBook-Pro:~ davidcartwright$ ssh dsc2@192.168.1.186
dsc2@192.168.1.186's password:
Last login: Mon Jul 27 20:50:57 2015
tcshrc:/home/dsc2 %
```

As we'd expect, it has run .tcshrc and has ignored .cshrc. So now let's delete .tcshrc (nothing else changes):

```
Davids-MacBook-Pro:~ davidcartwright$ ssh dsc2@192.168.1.186
dsc2@192.168.1.186's password:
Last login: Mon Jul 27 20:51:26 2015 from 192.168.1.156
cshrc:/home/dsc2 %
```

As it should, the shell has failed to find .tcshrc and has run .cshrc instead.

COMPARISONS - SOME SIMPLE SCRIPTS

We've had a look at what the shells do when you start them, but what are we actually putting in those configuration files? Answer: we're putting a collection of shell commands – commands that tell the shell to do stuff. In our case, each of the config files had a simple command that set the command prompt. So in our bash `.profile` we had:

```
PS1='profile@\t:\w\$ '
```

And in our tcsh `.cshrc` we had:

```
set prompt = cshrc:'${cwd}\ \%\ '
```

We won't go into precisely what these commands mean; suffice to say that the power of a shell is that it does way more than provide you with a way to execute command programs.

Command Program

By a command program, we mean something like `df` – the command that summarizes disk space usage. It feels like the shell is running the command but all it's actually doing is running a program called df that's located, in the case of our test machine, in directory /usr/bin. The shell is doing nothing but telling the program to run. The shell does, however, have a whole load of built-in commands and directives that allow you to do useful stuff. As well as just running one-off commands, you can tell the shell to do clever things. In this example, we'll use tcsh to enumerate all the files in a directory called 'files' and write the filename to the terminal:

```
cshrc:${cwd} % foreach i (`ls files`)
foreach? echo $i
foreach? end
1
2
3
```

The `foreach` command, as it suggests, executes something for each of the items in the list you throw at it (in this case, the output from the command `ls files` which catalogues the content of the directory 'files'). The `echo` command writes the name to the terminal, and `end` tells it we've finished writing the loop. Of course, we can do the same thing in bash:

```
[dsc@localhost Documents]$ for i in $(ls files); do
> echo $i
> done
1
2
3
```

The neat thing with shells is that you can take these commands and write programs – files full of commands that string loads of functions together to produce what, in many cases, are complicated results. These programs – the files full of shell commands – are called scripts. You can do anything in a script that you can do on the command line. So we can express the two functions we've just seen as scripts. We'll call the tcsh one `files.tcsh`:

```
foreach i (`ls files`)
  echo $i from the tcsh script
end
```

... and the bash one `files.bash`:

```
for i in $(ls files); do
  echo $i from the bash script
done
```

Hot Tip

Play with some scripts and get to grips with how they work; they're a great way to automate stuff you'd otherwise do by hand frequently.

As you'll see from the `echo` lines, we've embellished slightly so we can see which version's running. To run them, we start a new instance of the shell and pass it the name of the script we want to run.

```
                        dsc@linuxpc-local:~                          x
File  Edit  View  Search  Terminal  Help
[dsc@linuxpc-local ~]$ tcsh files.tcsh
1 from the tcsh script
2 from the tcsh script
3 from the tcsh script
[dsc@linuxpc-local ~]$ bash files.bash
1 from the bash script
2 from the bash script
3 from the bash script
[dsc@linuxpc-local ~]$ ▌
```

Above: The tsch and bash scripts running.

```
[dsc@localhost Documents]$ tcsh files.tcsh
1 from the tcsh script
2 from the tcsh script
3 from the tcsh script

[dsc@localhost Documents]$ bash files.bash
1 from the bash script
2 from the bash script
3 from the bash script
```

Writing Scripts

When it comes to shell commands, then, you can do powerful things. We've just scratched the surface here, but you can write scripts that call other scripts and do complex interactions – reading data from files, writing output to files and using variables to do calculations and string manipulation. The only downside with shells is that if you're used to one type and you're forced to use a different one, there's a bit of learning to do, because as we've seen, the syntax does vary. So if we try to run our tcsh script from above with bash, it'll blow up:

```
profile@21:37:01:~/Documents$ bash files.tcsh
files.tcsh: line 1: syntax error near unexpected token `('
files.tcsh: line 1: `foreach i (`ls files`)'
```

But don't fret, as we've seen there's a lot of similarity between shells too. So if we try to run our bash script from ksh:

```
profile@21:38:58:~/Documents$ ksh files.bash
1 from the bash script
2 from the bash script
3 from the bash script
```

It's perfectly happy because the set of commands and the syntax we happened to use in the bash script are common to bash and ksh.

Hot Tip

Ask Google to tell you about the 'shebang' or 'magic line' – it's a way of forcing the system to use the right shell to run a script.

THE IMPORTANT THING ABOUT SHELLS

It doesn't actually matter that much which shell you use. In reality, the functionality is largely the same, albeit with a few bells and whistles and a significant difference in command and script syntax between the csh family and the sh family. When it comes to scripting, then, unless you're a rocket scientist, there's little you can do in one shell that you can't do in another.

And which should you go for? If you're starting out, then the sh family – mainly bash – would be the sensible choice. The sh-style shells have cribbed most of the cool features of the csh family anyway, and given that all the start-up scripts are sh-based too, it's where the smart money goes when you're starting up in Linux shells.

GETTING STARTED

DOWNLOADING YOUR CHOSEN DISTRO

If you're a reader of one of the popular Linux magazines, then you'll often find one or more Linux distros on the DVD that comes with each issue. It's very likely, though, that it's not the one you'd prefer to use – so you'll want to go out and get the one you want.

For the commercial offerings from the likes of Red Hat and SUSE, you'll have to stump up real money; both of these have online shops. For the free offerings, it's just a case of navigating to the distro's website and downloading the one you want.

Below: It is wise to read up on a distro before committing to it.

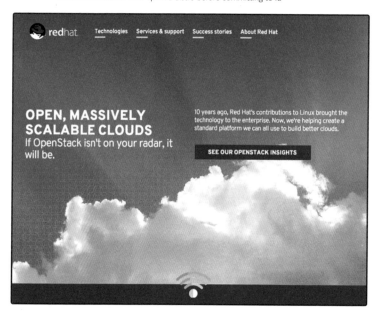

WHERE TO GO

Of the distros we've mentioned already, here's where to go and look:

- **Red Hat Enterprise Linux**: www.redhat.com/en

- **Fedora**: www.getfedora.org

- **CentOS**: www.centos.org

- **SUSE (commercial version):** www.suse.com

- **openSUSE:** www.opensuse.org/en

- **Ubuntu:** www.ubuntu.com

- **Debian:** www.debian.org

Hot Tip

We prefer to use 'Live' images – those that boot a whole Linux instead of just a minimal installer. You get more flexibility that way.

The usual way of installing Linux is to download the basic installer image and booting it from a DVD or USB key (we prefer USB – it's so much more convenient and it's no harder than creating a DVD image). The basic installer image isn't a complete set of installer files. Instead, it just has enough code crammed in to be able to boot most machines, display an installer GUI on the screen, configure the network (either cabled or wireless) and then download the rest of the options you've chosen via the internet. It does rely on you having a decent speed internet connection, but these days, that's seldom a problem.

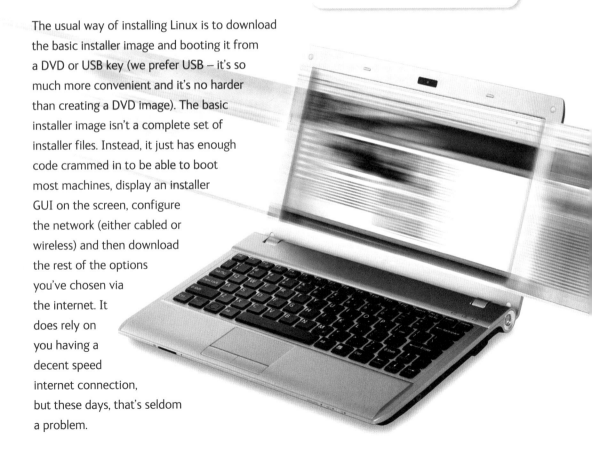

OUR CHOICE

For our test machine, we're downloading Fedora – specifically release 22. This came out in May 2015 – so at the time of writing, it's a couple of months old. This is about the minimum age we'd consider using for a Linux machine that's not running critical applications (in this case, it's for one of our laptops). If you're a business and you need to guarantee stability, you'd probably go for the previous version, as there will have been more bug fixes for the various components. In the case of Fedora, release 21 is about seven months old, which is about right. We'll stick with release 22 for our purposes though.

GETTING THE INSTALLER

Step one: go to the Fedora home page at www.getfedora.org. Incidentally, we're doing the download on a PC running Windows 8.1.

Below: The Fedora home page is very simple to use.

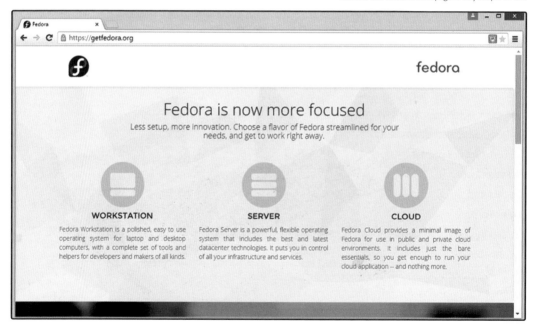

There are three options – Workstation, Server and Cloud – and we'll go for the Workstation option for this example.

There's a big, friendly 'Download now' link, so let's click that. We land on a page that lets us choose which particular installer we want. It's decided that the 64-bit 1.3GB Live Image is probably the one we want, and has put that by the 'Download' button at the top of the page.

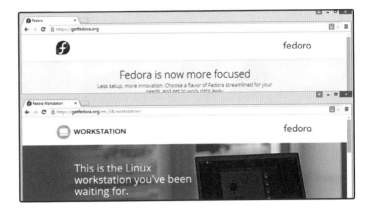

Above: Click on Workstation on the home page and the workstation download page will load.

If you look down the right-hand side, you'll see some other alternatives. There's a 32-bit Live Image, plus two 'netinstall' images – one 32-bit and the other 64-bit. Since the machine we're using is indeed a 64-bit PC, and we want to use the Live image, we'll simply click 'Download'. On our internet connection, the download runs at around 2MB per second, so it's just a few minutes' wait for the 1.3GB installer to download.

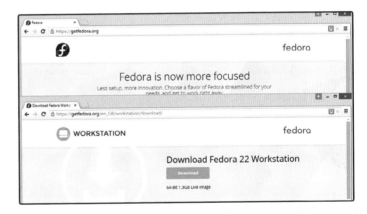

Above: If you're happy with the 64-bit 1.3GB Live Image, click on the download link to get started.

Hot Tip

Make sure you pick the right version (32 or 64 bit) – the download page may auto-detect your PC type but that's just the one you're downloading it to, which might be different from the one you're installing Linux on.

MAKING THE BOOTABLE DRIVE

1. The file that's just downloaded is an ISO image – basically a binary file that's an exact replica of a CD or DVD. You could therefore use a package like Nero to burn it to a disc, but in our case, we've decided to use a USB stick. Ours is a Kingston DataTraveler G3, a 32GB stick. The first thing we'll do is format it to ensure it's blank, using Windows' format utility – just go to the Computer icon (see below).

Below: Locate the computer icon of the USB stick under 'Devices and Drives'.

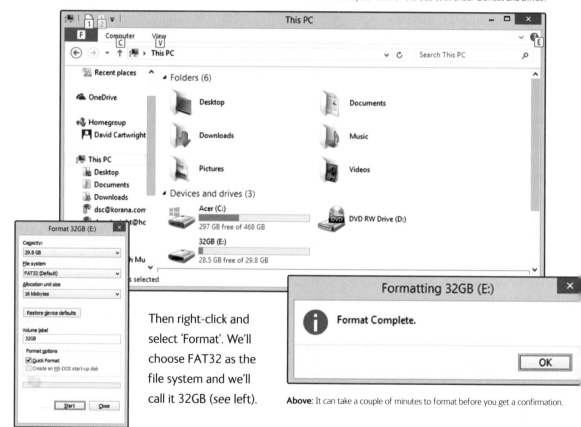

Above: Choose a File system and a Volume label before clicking Start.

Then right-click and select 'Format'. We'll choose FAT32 as the file system and we'll call it 32GB (see left).

Above: It can take a couple of minutes to format before you get a confirmation.

2. Once we've hit 'Start' and have confirmed that we really want to format the device, it takes a few seconds before confirming that it's done (see above).

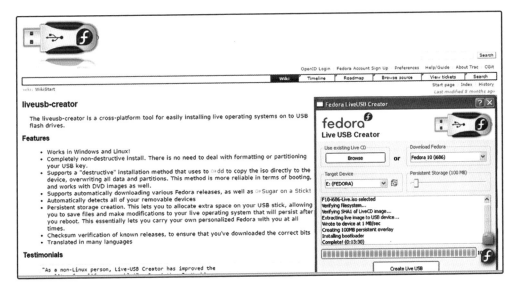

Above: This LiveUSB Creator will put the Fedora installer on to the USB stick.

3. Now all we need is a program that will write the ISO image of the Fedora installer to the stick. The recommended way to do this is using LiveUSB Creator, which is a free tool you can download from the internet: fedorahosted.org/liveusb-creator/

4. Scroll down the page a little and the link for the Windows version is there. It's about a 12MB download, so it shouldn't take long to pull down. The file is a Windows installer, so open it. Click Next (*see* right).

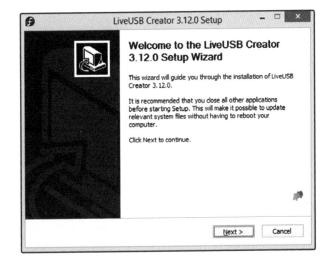

Above: Once you have opened the installer, this page will appear.

There's no need to change the install directory, so just click 'Install' and let it run through. Once it's finished, click 'Next' and you'll be on the final screen (*see left*).

5. Make sure the 'Run LiveUSB Creator' box is ticked and hit 'Finish'. The program will pop up after a few seconds (*see below*).

Right: Once it has started up, the LiveUSB Creator will show this screen.

6. To copy the Fedora image to the USB stick, we simply click 'Browse' and navigate to the image we downloaded, and make sure the Target Device is the stick we just formatted (*see right*).

7. Now all we have to do is hit 'Create Live USB' and wait. It's only a 1.3MB file, so two or three minutes is normal. Once it's finished, you can close the Creator app.

Below: The Fedora installer has now been successfully written to the USB stick.

Hot Tip

Keep a nice big USB stick to hand for stuff like this. They're relatively cheap and it's such a pain to run to the shop because you don't have a spare one when you need it.

RUNNING THE INSTALLER

Above: The Fedora welcome screen gives you the option of testing Fedora before installing.

What we now have is a USB stick that can boot our computer. Now, you may have to change the settings on your machine's start-up in the BIOS so it tries booting from the USB port before using its internal hard disk. That's something you'll have to Google for or check in your PC's documentation, as it varies from machine to machine.

Once you've sorted out the boot options for your PC, you should be able to fire it up with the stick inserted. You should see a black screen with a handful of options including 'Test this media & start Fedora Live'.

That's the default option, so just wait and it'll fire up. After a short while, you should see the Welcome to Fedora screen, which has two options: 'Try Fedora' and 'Install to Hard Drive' (see below).

Now, we want to install, but before we do so, we need to connect to a network so the installer can download its files. In our case, we'll use a wireless network.

Above: The utility menu indicates that WiFi has not yet been configured.

Above: The system produces a list of available wireless networks.

Above: Enter the WiFi password when prompted.

CONNECTING TO WIFI

1. To get to the WiFi config page, go to the top right and click the little triangle. A summary pop-up will appear, showing some basic information about Bluetooth and battery power but, more importantly, that the WiFi isn't yet connected (*see right*).

2. Click on the 'Not Connected' link and the system will scan for available wireless networks; after a few seconds, you'll get a list.

   Click on the one you want, and it'll ask you for the security key.

   Assuming you don't have finger trouble, it'll confirm that you're connected.

3. Now we've got the WiFi connection sorted, we can install. Click the Activities menu at the top left, and you'll see the 'Install to Hard Drive' option towards the bottom. Click this and the installer window will appear after a few seconds.

Hot Tip

Linux installers are pretty friendly these days, but check each screen carefully to make sure you haven't missed a setting.

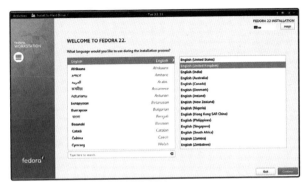

Above: The first step is to set your language.

This is a fairly simple wizard. On the first screen you'll choose your language and variation; we'll go for English, and the United Kingdom (*see* top).

4. Click 'Continue' and it'll think about your system for a moment; in our case, we've selected the WiFi network already – the only warning we see is for the Installation Destination (*see* right).

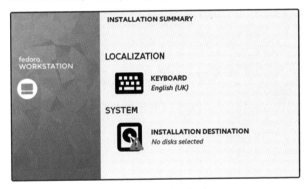

Above: Here, the Installation Destination still needs to be set.

So let's click that. On our PC, we have a couple of options. Now, the SanDisk Cruzer is actually a USB stick that we're using to capture the screenshots we're using here – we need to select the 931.51GiB ATA disk.

Click it and a little tick appears (*see* bottom right). Then click 'Done'.

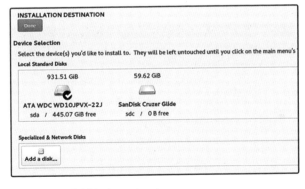

Above: The install disk has been selected.

Above: No error messages means it's now possible to start installation.

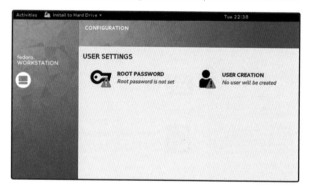

Above: An icon with an exclamation point shows that no root user password has been set.

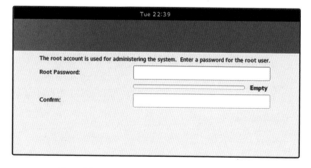

Above: The root password can be used to administer the system.

5. Now we're back at the installer main screen with no warnings. The Begin Installation button is enabled, so let's click it.

6. The installer will now spend quite a while installing the software. In the meantime, there are a couple of things you can do. You'll see that it's warning you that there's no root password set (*see middle left*).

Click on the icon and you'll be prompted to set a password (make sure you choose a decent, secure one – it'll warn you if the one you choose is too obvious).

Click 'Done' when you're finished. You ought also to create a normal user account – click on 'User Creation' and enter the user's real name, the login ID you want to use, and a password.

After several minutes of chugging, the installer will finish (you can watch the progress bar to see how it's doing), see below.

7. Hit 'Quit' and the installer will exit. Now all you have to do is click the triangle in the top right, hit the On/Off icon, and select 'Restart'. Remember once the screen's gone black to pull out the USB stick you booted from, and you should see your PC boot into its freshly installed Linux set-up.

Hot Tip

If you wish, you can 'dual boot' your PC – that is, have Windows and Linux both installed and select the one you want at boot time. Get the hang of installing Linux on its own first though.

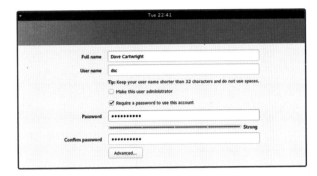

Above: You should always log into your Linux machine as a normal user, not the root super user.

Above: While Fedora is installing, you can set a password and create a user account.

Above: Fedora has successfully installed.

NEXT STEPS

Once you've installed Linux, you have a working system, but not one that's up to date. The makers of the distros don't constantly change their installer image whenever a new tweak to something comes out; after release 22 of Fedora, for instance, the next image you'll see is release 23.

WHAT SHOULD YOU BE LOOKING FOR?

So just as you do when you install any other operating system – Mac OS or Windows, for example – the first thing to do is make sure you get everything up to date. This is really easy to do, as we'll see in a moment.

Why do we run the upgrade straight away? Easy – we always want to start with a system that's bang up to date (we'll get back to managing regular updates later).

Different distros have different package managers, and hence different ways of running updates. As of release 22, Fedora have actually changed their package manager from Yum to one called DNF. It's dead easy to use though – just run `dnf update`:

```
[root@localhost ~]# dnf update
Fedora 22 - x86_64 - Updates        998 kB/s |   13 MB        00:13
Last metadata expiration check performed 0:00:09 ago on Sat Aug
1 17:04:41 2015.
Dependencies resolved.

=====================================================
 Package        Arch        Version        Repository        Size
=====================================================
Installing:
 drpm        x86_64        0.2.0-2.fc22        updates        30 k
 kernel        x86_64        4.1.3-200.fc22        updates        67 k
 kernel-core        x86_64        4.1.3-200.fc22        updates        19 M
 kernel-modules        x86_64        4.1.3-200.fc22        updates        133 k
 PackageKit-gstreamer-plugin  x86_64 1.0.6-6.fc22  updates   20 k
 PackageKit-gtk3-module        x86_64        1.0.6-6.fc22        updates        21 k
 SDL2        x86_64        2.0.3-5.fc22        updates        361 k
 abrt        x86_64        2.6.1-2.fc22        updates        518 k
 abrt-addon-ccpp        x86_64        2.6.1-2.fc22        updates        187 k
 xorg-x11-server-Xorg        x86_64        1.17.2-2.fc22        updates        1.4 M
 xorg-x11-server-Xwayland  x86_64  1.17.2-2.fc22  updates  914 k
 xorg-x11-server-common  x86_64  1.17.2-2.fc22  updates  44 k
 zenity        x86_64        3.16.3-1.fc22        updates        3.4 M
 zip        x86_64        3.0-14.fc22        updates        267 k
Transaction Summary
=====================================================

Install    10 Packages
Upgrade    522 Packages
Total download size: 715 M
Is this ok [y/N]:
```

We've pruned this list because, as you can see, it wants to upgrade 522 packages (and it listed each one individually). This sounds like a big deal, but actually it isn't – in all but the rarest cases, you just leave it to trot along. As you can see, it's telling us that there's 715MB of data to download and asking us if that's okay. We'll say yes by answering 'y'.

```
Total download size: 715 M
Is this ok [y/N]: y
```

The installer keeps us up to date with progress as it downloads things:

```
Downloading Packages:
(1/532): drpm-0.2.0-2.fc22.x86_64.rpm   238 kB/s | 30 kB    00:00
(2/532): kernel-4.1.3-200.fc22.x86_64.rpm   275 kB/s | 67 kB 00:00
(3/532): python-firewall-0.3.14.2-2.fc22.noarch.rpm 582 kB/s | 236 kB 00:00
(4/532): systemd-compat-libs-219-20.fc22.x86_64.rpm 498 kB/s | 135 kB 00:00
```

... and so on. And once downloaded, it keeps us updated on progress with the installation of packages:

```
Running transaction check
Transaction check succeeded.
Running transaction test
Transaction test succeeded.
Running transaction
  Upgrading : libgcc-5.1.1-4.fc22.x86_64                1/1055
  Upgrading : fontpackages-filesystem-1.44-12.fc22.noarch    2/1055
  Upgrading : google-noto-fonts-common-20150417-1.fc22.noarch  3/1055
  Upgrading : dejavu-fonts-common-2.35-1.fc22.noarch      4/1055
```

... and so on.

One thing you may notice when it's installing things is that it doesn't normally install items in the same order that it downloaded them in. This is because many programs are split into multiple packages instead of coming down as one big chunk, and the packages have interdependencies – that is, some of them have to be installed before others. We'll come back to that general point later when we talk about programs.

CHOOSING YOUR PROGRAMS

OK, so we now have a working system that's nicely up to date. Now it's time to decide what programs we actually want to run on it.

One of the things with the open source world is that there are often several alternatives when it comes to choosing the programs you adopt. So, for instance, if you want an email system, you have loads of options, of which the two popular ones are Postfix and Sendmail. Similarly, if you want a database system, you'll probably choose between MariaDB (the new alternative to the famous MySQL package) and PostgreSQL.

Do you have to choose, or can you actually run two systems side by side? The answer is that it depends. For an email server package, you need to choose one and stick with it: because mail software 'listens' for incoming connections in a particular way, only one program can be listening at any one time. But for databases and many other packages, you're perfectly okay to run two or more equivalents side by side – though, of course, we'd always recommend picking one and sticking with it, because it saves having to learn several systems.

STICK WITH PACKAGES WHERE POSSIBLE

Sometimes, you'll come across programs that haven't been made into official packages for the particular Linux distro you've chosen. Of course open source software is available in a form where you can download and build it yourself, but this is strictly not for beginners. Although software authors go to great pains to make the build process as easy as possible, you'll still often come across error messages that are cryptic and not covered by the installation documentation, which means you spend more time Googling and hoping someone else has seen that problem than installing and using the programs.

So unless you really have to use a particular package and it's worth the grief of a self-build process, stick with programs that you can install from prebuilt packages.

Hot Tip

Packages are great, because someone else has figured out all the tricky stuff about building them. Make the most of their hard work!

PROGRAM DEPENDENCIES

We mentioned earlier that packages often depend on each other. Let's take an example –
the PHP system (a web-page scripting language that you'll probably use at some point if
you ever build a Linux-based website). Let's run the command to install the PHP program,
dnf install php:

```
[root@localhost ~]# dnf install php
Last metadata expiration check performed 0:35:26 ago on Sat Aug  1
17:04:41 2015.
Dependencies resolved.
================================================================================
 Package          Arch          Version          Repository          Size
================================================================================
Installing:
 php          x86_64          5.6.11-2.fc22          updates          2.6 M
 php-cli          x86_64          5.6.11-2.fc22          updates          4.0 M
 php-common          x86_64          5.6.11-2.fc22          updates          1.1 M
 php-pecl-jsonc          x86_64          1.3.7-1.fc22          fedora          57 k
Transaction Summary
================================================================================
Install   4 Packages
Total download size: 7.8 M
Installed size: 29 M
Is this ok [y/N]:
```

As you'll see, the DNF package manager has found a package called PHP. It has, however,
checked the dependencies of that package and has found three others that it knows it'll need
to install in order for PHP to work. All we have to do is confirm that we want to perform the
installation, and within five minutes or so, we have the program and the things it relies on
installed and ready to go.

KEEPING PROGRAMS UP TO DATE

When we installed Linux, the first thing we did once we'd finished was run the updater to ensure that all the elements of the system were the most recent versions. But all we did was give it a basic instruction: 'Go and find updates for anything that's installed.'

You could, of course, do the same thing once every week or so to ensure everything was up to date. And if you're running Linux on your desktop machine at home and you don't mind the occasional problem, then there's nothing preventing you from doing so. But say you're doing something that needs a bit more reliability – perhaps you've decided to run up your first Linux server so it can run your website. You probably want to be a bit more discriminatory.

Changing Functionality or Security

Generally speaking, updates to a Linux machine work correctly without crashing. But that correct behaviour might be different from how it used to work. Software marches on, and although there are updates that fix bugs and make it work better, there are also often updates that change the functionality because the way something was designed has been superseded by a more efficient alternative or, more often, a security fix. Let's take an example of something used all over the world – the PHP web development language we mentioned earlier. Read the page on the PHP home site that discusses, say, migrating from version 5.5 to version 5.6 and you'll see a couple of

Hot Tip
When you first install, you can do an 'update all', but be more picky once your machine is in general use, in case you break something.

deprecated features with the words 'Support for these calls will be removed in a future version of PHP'. So you need to be careful about running updates on Linux machines whose functionality you care about.

Screening Updates

The approach you should take is simple. Run the package manager's 'check if there are updates available' command (with DNF, this would be `dnf check-update`). Then run down the list of items that it's telling you are available for updating, and make a note of the ones that relate to core components you rely heavily on. It'll tell you the version it's planning to upgrade to, and you can ask the package manager to show you the version that's currently installed (with DNF, that's `dnf list installed`). You then just need to check on the home page for the various apps you care about most, so you can understand whether changing versions will break your world (or, more likely, introduce a change that will work for the next few versions but will eventually be removed).

Updating CUPS

Once you've decided which items to update, name them to the package manager. So in this example, we'll update CUPS (the printing core of Linux). According to `dnf list installed` we presently have version 2.0.2-5, and according to `dnf check-update` the current release is 2.0.3-1. So we'll use DNF to update it:

Hot Tip

Again, the package manager is your friend. Remember that as well as installing and updating, it can also uninstall stuff you don't want.

```
[root@localhost ~]# dnf upgrade cups
Last metadata expiration check performed 0:03:17 ago on Sat Aug  1
19:45:51 2015.
Dependencies resolved.
========================================================
 Package          Arch          Version          Repository          Size
========================================================
Upgrading:
 cups         x86_64         1:2.0.3-1.fc22         updates         1.3 M
 cups-client         x86_64         1:2.0.3-1.fc22         updates         153 k
 cups-filesystem         noarch         1:2.0.3-1.fc22         updates         99 k
 cups-libs         x86_64         1:2.0.3-1.fc22         updates         387 k
Transaction Summary
================================================
Upgrade  4 Packages
Total download size: 2.0 M
Is this ok [y/N]:
```

Oh, and if you're wondering why we've used the upgrade directive instead of the update one we used earlier: they do the same thing, but the authors seem to have preserved the upgrade directive, as it's familiar to anyone who's used to the Yum package manager.

Controlled updates of this kind will keep your Linux platform stable.

DO I WANT ANOTHER DESKTOP MANAGER?

We've already mentioned that there tend to be several alternatives of programs that can do anything you want on Linux. And one of the key options is the desktop environment that presents the GUI interface on your Linux machine. On our test machine the Gnome desktop was installed by default, but you have plenty of options.

Because desktop environments are complex beasts, they're implemented as 'package groups' in Linux. So if we run `dnf grouplist`, it'll tell us what we have available:

```
[root@localhost ~]# dnf grouplist
Last metadata expiration check performed 0:31:12 ago on Sat Aug 1 19:45:51 2015.
Available environment groups:
    Minimal Install
    Fedora Server
    Fedora Workstation
    Fedora Cloud Server
    KDE Plasma Workspaces
    Xfce Desktop
    LXDE Desktop
```

> **Hot Tip**
>
> Desktop environments can be quite sizeable, so don't just download them and leave them lying around when you're not using them.

This is a truncated list, by the way. If we want to install KDE, we'd run `dnf groupinstall KDE Plasma Workspaces`. And similarly, to install the Xfce desktop, we'd run `dnf groupinstall Xfce Desktop`.

We chose Xfce, which took about five minutes to download and install. Once you've downloaded it, though, you need to tell the system to use it. This is a simple case of running the `switchdesk` utility (note that you'll have to install the switchdesk package first – you should be able by now to figure out how to do that):

```
[root@localhost ~]# switchdesk xfce
Red Hat Linux switchdesk 4.0
Copyright (C) 1999-2010 Red Hat, Inc
Redistributable under the terms of the GNU General Public License
Desktop now set up to run xfce.
```

Interestingly, you can see Fedora's heritage in the output of switchdesk, with the mention of Red Hat as the original producer.

ISSUES TO BEAR IN MIND

We've walked through the process of going from a bare system to a working Linux machine, and the result should be pretty impressive – a working machine with an attractive user interface (they're all pretty good straight out of the box) which is able to communicate with your other computers, surf the internet and run the applications you want to use. This is the real world, however, and there are a few things you need to have in mind when you're installing and using Linux for real.

IS IT REAL?

One thing we didn't mention in the section about downloading the Linux distribution is that whenever you download any open source file you should make sure that the image you download is genuine. If you're working from the official website then it's usually fine, but you should check. You do this using a thing called a checksum – this is calculated by a program that takes every byte of a file and performs a calculation that results in a string of characters. The idea is that only that file will have that string calculated as its checksum.

Let's take our Fedora image as an example of how to check the integrity of the file. If we look in the directory where the installer file lives on the Fedora website, we see a number of files:

- Fedora-Live-Workstation-x86_64-22-3.iso
- Fedora-Workstation-22-x86_64-CHECKSUM
- Fedora-Workstation-netinst-x86_64-22.iso

The Fedora-Live-Workstation-x86_64-22-3.iso file is the image we downloaded and used to install Linux. But if we download the Fedora-Workstation-22-x86_64-CHECKSUM file – which is very small – and check its contents, we see a cryptic message:

```
—-BEGIN PGP SIGNED MESSAGE—-
Hash: SHA256

# The image checksum(s) are generated with sha256sum.
SHA256 (Fedora-Workstation-netinst-x86_64-22.iso) =
c9d22e708b21336582b19b336b7063fc4b882be4cf96d4d0693de07bd66c25e8
SHA256 (Fedora-Live-Workstation-x86_64-22-3.iso) =
615abfc89709a46a078dd1d39638019aa66f62b0ff8325334f1af100551bb6cf
—-BEGIN PGP SIGNATURE—-
Version: GnuPG v1

iQIcBAEBCAAGBQJVX4e1AAoJEBGtwJSOFDHV4CoQAJPVhYeO5m7cyYQP9T0T9qVH
GpMTWGOdMGAdPpinFbCQTquTI2jMeoqP5LxQy8QADS5FcVQmnTLQzBXqvxCwa/xv
6mS+VCsfgoYPoY4tUum4Q9q3EwBD0DgY/vrCcdNQqaxMLmUVi9baz2Rm14lyDYDB
Oa4dAmL9tm5LCBRLqEHTlk99yvPb02L0uRZUeBZFf+tEiaimjBdXnO8ppi3PjHtJ
saBDOZnVzjn3ZJfSJ0M8HGmG3yFiDyRoH04GyiBU27C+kr8q7pTMcrwYb1TqT2kP
—-END PGP SIGNATURE—-
```

See at the top where it says Hash: SHA256? It's telling us that the type of checksum is the Secure Hash Algorithm. It also tells us that the checksum for our installer file is:

```
615abfc89709a46a078dd1d39638019aa66f62b0ff8325334f1af100551bb6cf
```

So if we calculate the SHA256 checksum for our ISO image, we should get this same sequence. On our Mac, we do this with the shasum command:

```
DCPro: davidcartwright$ shasum -a 256 Fedora-Live-Workstation-
x86_64-22-3.iso
615abfc89709a46a078dd1d39638019aa66f62b0ff8325334f1af100551bb6cf
       Fedora-Live-Workstation-x86_64-22-3.iso
```

Hot Tip

Always check the integrity of anything you're going to install. As well as confirming validity, it shows that the download finished okay and there's nothing missing.

And sure enough, there's our matching checksum. Not only does this tell us it's a genuine file, but it's also a handy check that the file is complete. If you want to check the SHA checksum using Windows, there are various options – such as the free one at www.raylin.wordpress.com /downloads/md5-sha-1-checksum-utility/. As we've mentioned, don't just do

Below: Checking the SHA checksum is a very good practice to pick up.

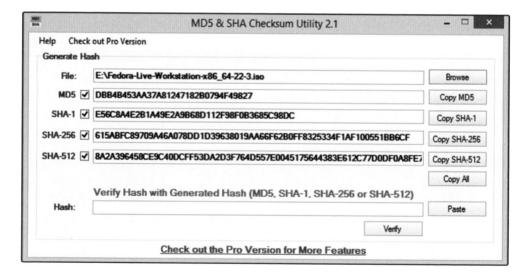

this for the Linux installer – do it for any open source file you download. You don't often get dodgy files if you're using the official website, but you should always check, just in case.

BACKING UP YOUR COMPUTER

You've gone to all the effort of getting your computer up and running on Linux, and so you ought really to back up your data once you've done so. With some platforms, you can do cunning things like syncing the local computer disk with a remote storage area in the Cloud (we back up our Mac via an automated sync with Google Drive, for instance) but as we'll see in a short while, this isn't necessarily an option for Linux.

What you can do though, is use the 'Backup-Manager' tool to hive important files off to a remote file store – either a USB-connected disk or, more likely, a shared folder on another machine that the Linux computer can mount over the network.

Installing Backup-Manager

Installing Backup-Manager is a simple DNF command as usual:

```
[root@localhost desktop-integration]# dnf install backup-manager
```

The precise configuration depends on what you want to back up – as usual, check out the man page. This has a pointer to the author's website where you can find more detailed documentation.

The main question to ask is what to back up. Given that all (or at least most) of your applications have been installed using the package manager, there's not really a lot of point backing up the individual files that make up the application installs. The main motivation for wanting to back up the

Hot Tip

Backups are essential: most of us have been bitten by our PC crashing and have lost something we'd have liked to keep hold of.

computer is to recover the data in the event that the machine becomes completely unusable –
if the disk becomes corrupted, for example. The most sensible way to work is often to decide
that in the event of a complete crash, it's probably easier to reinstall Linux from scratch (we
can do it in less than an hour, and so can you now you have the tutorial). So you'll concentrate
the Backup-Manager configuration on your data files and perhaps some of the configuration
files for key applications.

SOME STUFF STILL ISN'T POSSIBLE

In Linux's very early days, it was common to find that it lagged behind other platforms –
primarily Windows – when it came to applications being available to run on it and for drivers
to be available for new pieces of computer hardware. Over the years, this has become less and
less the case – Linux is now such a mainstream operating system that equipment vendors
consider it a normal part of their driver development task when they release new hardware.

Below: Google Drive can be very useful for accessing your files wherever you are.

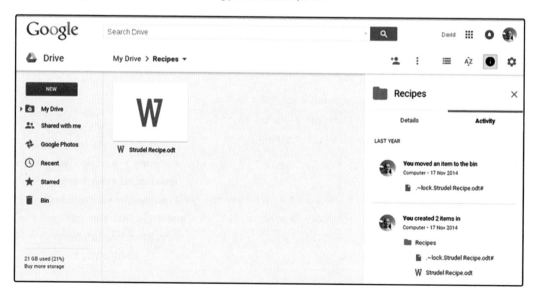

However, this doesn't mean that it's universally accepted and supported by all the vendors out there. So for example, because we've just been looking at how to back up your machine, I was looking for alternatives for accessing Cloud-based storage on the Linux platform. Now, while the likes of Dropbox has a Linux version, the same can't be said for, say, Google Drive – which came as a surprise to us. Similarly, Citrix ShareFile and, perhaps less surprisingly, Apple's iCloud.

Google Drive

You can still use Cloud storage systems that don't have a Linux version. Let's take Google Drive as an example. On Windows and Mac you can automatically sync files between your local disk and the remote copy, as there's a desktop application for each of these platforms. On Linux you can't do that. What you can do, however, is use the service via the web browser. Although files don't automatically sync, you can at least download them easily to the local disk to work on them, then re-upload them by simply dragging them on to the web browser windows.

SOME STUFF ISN'T PACKAGED

We've mentioned previously that some software isn't packaged and you ought to try to avoid it. Sometimes, though, it's so useful that you want to make the effort.

Happily, unpackaged software isn't always an utter nightmare to install. If you're downloading the source code and compiling it yourself, this can be fraught with incomprehensible error messages and complaints from the compiler that one or more required components are missing so it can't continue. But in other cases, you find that the software provider has done a lot of the work for you. For instance, if you want to use the OpenOffice application suite, you download a bundle of package files from the producer's website and follow a relatively straightforward 'read me' instruction file to install the components.

Hot Tip

Be prepared to fiddle and to Google: the 'how to' documentation is usually good with unpackaged programs, but on your particular system, you may get error messages they don't cover.

COMPATIBILITY

Having discussed a moment ago the fact that some applications simply aren't available for Linux yet, it's worth considering how compatible your Linux machine is (or isn't) when it comes to making it work with other computers you own, or perhaps use at work.

Application Compatibility

Some applications just don't exist for Linux. Microsoft Office, for example; there's a Mac version and a Windows version, but no Linux flavour. In such cases, you need to rely on the ability of the applications you *do* have to open files using formats that are compatible with the other platforms you use. LibreOffice (the popular office suite for Linux) is able to open documents in Microsoft Office formats, though there's no guarantee that the formatting of, say, a Word 2013 document will be preserved absolutely correctly when you open it in LibreOffice.

Hot Tip

Linux software has been designed by people who want you to be able to deal with non-Linux documents, but compatibility isn't always 100%.

Below: Accessing your Mac files on your Linux computer is easy to do.

Network Interaction

Consider the ability to interact with other operating systems over the network, and in fact, this tends to be very simple because pretty much anything you own is likely to be able to communicate using Windows' basic file-sharing protocols. So for instance, it was very easy indeed to turn on file sharing on our Mac and navigate to it on the Linux computer.

Corporate Directory Service

Next is the more advanced functionality that you may have to use if looking to use Linux on a corporate network. The main requirement in this context is for Linux users to be able to authenticate against the corporate directory service – which nine times out of ten will be Microsoft Active Directory. The good news is that although traditionally quite tricky, this is perfectly feasible today; the bad news is that it's well out of the scope of someone who's just getting to grips with Linux, as there are lots of very cryptic-looking commands you need to run.

THE GUI IS YOUR FRIEND

You may have noticed that the illustrations we've used in this book fall into two categories. First are traditional screenshots, which show the graphical interface of modern Linux systems. Second, we have the text-based command snippets that we've used to show the commands that you can use regardless of whether you're running a graphical interface on your machine.

In the early days of Linux, with very limited memory and processing power, graphical user interfaces were not commonplace and were generally very tricky to get running. The same can't be said today, though, and so the normal way to use Linux – on a desktop computer anyway – is to use one of the desktop environments.

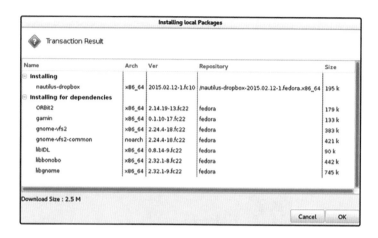

Name	Arch	Ver	Repository	Size
Installing local Packages				
Transaction Result				
Installing				
nautilus-dropbox	x86_64	2015.02.12-1.fc10	/nautilus-dropbox-2015.02.12-1.fedora.x86_64	195 k
Installing for dependencies				
ORBit2	x86_64	2.14.19-13.fc22	fedora	179 k
gamin	x86_64	0.1.10-17.fc22	fedora	133 k
gnome-vfs2	x86_64	2.24.4-18.fc22	fedora	383 k
gnome-vfs2-common	noarch	2.24.4-18.fc22	fedora	421 k
libIDL	x86_64	0.8.14-9.fc22	fedora	90 k
libbonobo	x86_64	2.32.1-8.fc22	fedora	442 k
libgnome	x86_64	2.32.1-9.fc22	fedora	745 k

Download Size : 2.5 M

Cancel   OK

So make the most of it. Yes, you can use the command line to, say, install software, but equally, there will be a graphical package manager on whatever Linux distro you've chosen. We used one to install the Dropbox client when we were researching the previous section, for instance.

Left: Here, the Dropbox client is installing using the graphical package manager.

IT CAN BE QUITE SECURE OUT OF THE BOX

The final thing to bear in mind is that Linux is regarded as a very secure, solid operating system. So if you're installing it from scratch, the chances are that your computer works fine when you're using the keyboard and screen, but that you can't connect to it from anywhere else.

Let's take an example. One of the fundamental features of Unix-like operating systems is the ability to connect from another computer and type commands at a shell window. But if we try to connect using the secure shell or ssh command to our test machine (in this case from a Mac), we're blocked:

```
DCPro:~ davidcartwright$ ssh dsc@192.168.1.186
ssh: connect to host 192.168.1.186 port 22: Connection refused
```

This is because, by default, Linux has its doors shut – we can't make connections until we've turned on the service that accepts them:

```
[root@localhost ~]# systemctl start sshd
```

Now we can try again to connect from the Mac:

```
DCPro:~ davidcartwright$ ssh dsc@192.168.1.186
The authenticity of host '192.168.1.186 (192.168.1.186)' can't
be established.
RSA key fingerprint is
77:72:78:b0:5b:f7:d1:02:ce:cd:44:e5:a5:92:7e:ed.
Are you sure you want to continue connecting (yes/no)? yes
Warning: Permanently added '192.168.1.186' (RSA) to the list
of known hosts.
dsc@192.168.1.186's password:
Last login: Sat Aug  1 22:24:59 2015
```

Success! Instead of throwing out the connection, we're asked whether we want to accept the security key, then after providing the right password, we're allowed in.

Additional Security

You may find that your chosen Linux comes with additional security items enabled that prevent remote access even when you've turned on the connectivity features, for example the IPTables firewall system. So if you can't get in even though you've ticked all the right boxes in the configuration, check that it doesn't have an unknown firewall running.

Hot Tip

SSHD is the first thing we turn on when we install Linux – it means we can all connect in and configure/install stuff in parallel.

WORKING WITH LINUX

HOW THE DIFFERENT DISTROS WORK

There are so many different Linux distros available that you'd think they can't all be the same – and, of course, you'd be right. This isn't a reference to the fact that some of the distros are available in flavours that support numerous different processor architectures though, since for a given distro, the different flavours look pretty much the same.

The differences are twofold. First is the way you install the product itself – from a 'slimline' image on a USB stick that gives you just enough to install the rest over the internet, up to a wallet full of DVDs that between them contain the entire suite of software you'll need. Second is the support model – from self-support up to business-class remote assistance from a 24/7 call centre.

WHAT FORM CAN YOU GET THEM IN?

Our first Linux installation – the Slackware one on page 27 – came from an internet download, which we wrote on to a stack of floppy disks. In this respect Linux started how it meant to go on. To this day, the majority of

Linux installations start life with a download from a website. This includes the commercial versions: RHEL is a downloadable product so long as you've got an active subscription and hence can log into the support portal; and similarly, SUSE's online shop tells us in the 'Stock Status' column of the product purchase page that it's an electronic download.

Hot Tip

We never bother with CD or DVD distros – a USB stick and a decent internet connection are fine by us.

Likewise when you go to an online retailer, the products you're buying aren't boxes containing CDs and manuals but online subscriptions – you'll simply receive some cryptic codes that you can then register by visiting the vendor's website. Why would a vendor bother with the expense of printing DVDs and manuals when so many of them will end up in landfill or the recycle bin once the next version has been released?

Below: You can download many different distros from their individual websites. This is Ubuntu's download page.

While there are CD-based versions of Linuxes, they tend to be produced by third parties, not the actual Linux distro makers themselves. So Amazon's US site will sell you a Linux Mint CD for $9.99, or you can get a bootable version on a USB stick from Amazon UK for £8.79. Oh, and, of course, if you keep an eye on the Linux magazines in your local newsagent, you'll usually find that the cover DVD has one or more distros on it.

Below: It's important to check the speed of your internet before you do a basic internet install.

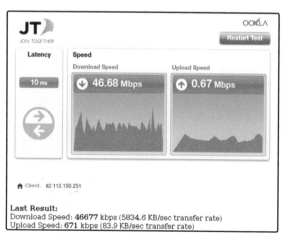

THE INSTALLATION MODEL

There are typically three installation models you can use, one of which you'll already have tried if you did the Fedora install that we went through earlier.

Basic Internet Install

With the basic network installation, you download a very, very small image and write it to a CD, DVD or USB stick. The idea is to boot the machine into a very basic image that's nice and small to download, and has just enough to get the machine up and running, connected to a network and give you a (hopefully) comprehensible user interface through which you can select your installation options.

The benefit of a basic internet install is that you don't need a big beefy USB stick to house the installer files, which is great if you're going to do a fairly customized installation with a small set of features (why download a gigabyte of stuff if you're only going to use a couple of hundred megs of it?). The downside is that unless you have some kind of cache server on your network, if you're doing a number of installations, you'll end up pulling data down from the internet again and again. If you're on a 50Mbit/s internet link like ours, that's fine, but if you have a broadband connection running at a few megabits, it can be painful even for a smallish install.

Live Install

The installation we did in our Fedora example used the Live install image. These are very common among distros, and they're an excellent compromise, because if you're doing a default install without trimming out the bells and whistles, it has all the files it needs on the install media. If you recall, when we did our walk-through we set the wireless LAN settings before doing the install. Actually we didn't have to do this, as everything it needed was on the USB stick anyway; we merely did it because it was a useful thing to do (and when the install was complete it wrote the wireless settings to the Linux installation so we were straight on the network when we rebooted).

Hot Tip

Live installs are our favourite – it lets you start up a pretty full Linux and gives more flexibility than a slimmed-down network install.

DVD Install

The final option is to download a bunch of ISO images but burn them to CDs or DVDs for use as installation media. This is about as close as you get to a 'traditional' installation method, so you can enjoy a nostalgic half hour of swapping discs when prompted to do so. We'd recommend against CDs for the larger distros, but DVDs are fine (Debian 8, for instance, uses 17 CDs including the updaters if you go for the full set, but only four DVDs).

SUPPORT OPTIONS

The final consideration in how the various distros work is the support model – how you get help in the event of a problem. And here, there are three options, of which the first isn't particularly supportive!

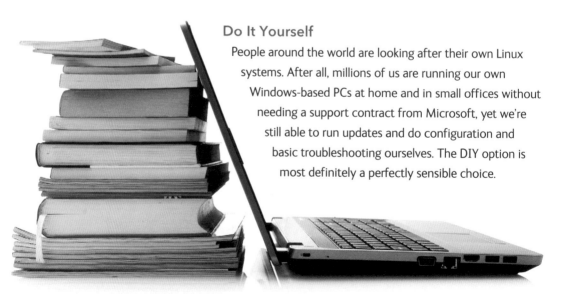

Do It Yourself

People around the world are looking after their own Linux systems. After all, millions of us are running our own Windows-based PCs at home and in small offices without needing a support contract from Microsoft, yet we're still able to run updates and do configuration and basic troubleshooting ourselves. The DIY option is most definitely a perfectly sensible choice.

Free Linux Plus a Consultant

This is a very popular option for small businesses that want to use open source Linux installations instead of splashing out on formal support for commercial Linux installations; when you have these in any number the costs do tend to become significant. There's still a thriving industry of small and medium-sized companies that do general IT support on a contract basis, for significantly less cost than a collection of commercial Linux subscriptions.

Hot Tip

Free Linux plus a consultant is a surprisingly good value way to go – and there are some great ones out there that you can pay just a modest retainer.

Commercial Support

Option three is to go for the paid-for commercial support. As we've seen when comparing the cost of a new small-business server with Windows and different commercial distros, Linux is actually more costly if you simply compare prices, but what you get is very impressive: Red Hat's basic support gets you a response within one business hour, for example, while SUSE's is largely similar (working-hours cover, with two-hour response). Pay more for the advanced option and you'll have 24/7 cover for system-down problems. It's not cheap, but the support you get is commensurate with what you're paying.

SIMILARITIES AND DIFFERENCES

Having noted that Linux distros come in different forms with regard to how you get them, install them and support them, the other side of the coin is the distribution you use. All distros have some features in common – the core elements that make them Linux rather than anything else. But there wouldn't be a need for so many distros if they didn't all have their distinguishing features.

WAS IT A GOOD YEAR?

We've told you a bit about the Linux makers, but let's have a brief amble through the chronology of the various Linux distros we've discussed throughout these pages.

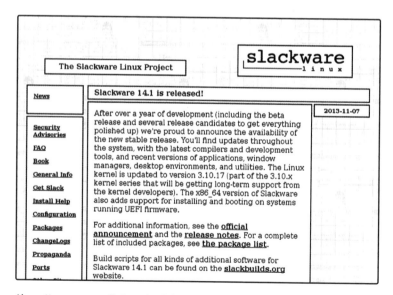

Above: Here you can see Slackware. It isn't the prettiest but it is one of the founding fathers of Linux.

Slackware

Slackware was the first Linux we came across. One of the authors worked as a Sun system administrator in academic IT when it arrived in June 1993, which gave the benefit of a half-decent connection to the internet (still a fledgling concept in those days) and an unlimited supply of 1.44MB floppy disks. Configuring Slackware was neither quick nor pretty, but it worked.

SUSE

While we're on the subject of Slackware we can't fail to mention SuSE (whose 'U' magically became capitalized over the years – we'll use the fully capitalized version to avoid confusion). Why? Because Slackware was a 'tidied up' version of a thing called SLS that originated in 1992; SUSE 4.2 (the first incarnation, despite the number) was a German translation of Slackware.

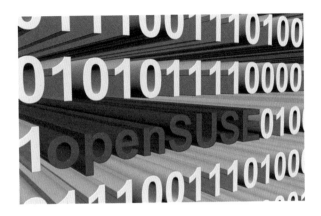

Debian

Of a similar vintage is Debian, whose initial incarnation also winked into existence in 1993, thanks to the efforts of a single developer, though as with other versions, the community grew and made it what it is today. Although perhaps overshadowed these days by some of the better-known distros, it was there right at the start.

Red Hat

Just a couple of years on, May 1995 saw the advent of Red Hat Linux 1.0; the product we know today had the word 'Enterprise' added in March 2002 with the advent of RHEL 2.1 on general release and the realization that Linux stood a chance of being taken seriously as a corporate operating system.

CentOS

CentOS emerged in the spring of 2004 and comes from RHEL stock, and continues to be based on the new RHEL releases as they come out. The writers go to great pains to point out that CentOS isn't simply a free copy of RHEL, but that said, it's built on open source code made available by Red Hat, and the project board for CentOS includes Red Hat people.

Fedora

Heading down the Fedora line from a similar RHEL heritage, Fedora Core 1 (the first half dozen or so releases were all Fedora Core something) came out in November 2003. And *quelle surprise* – Fedora also has formal sponsorship and input from the team at Red Hat.

Ubuntu

Around 2004, we have the arrival of Ubuntu, the first official release of which was confusingly numbered 4.1. Although, as we've mentioned, Ubuntu has tight links with Canonical, it's nonetheless a proper community-driven Linux implementation.

Below: An Ubuntu desktop.

Developments in the Last Decade

Finally, in 2004 came the SUSE embarkation into an open version, with the arrival of OpenSUSE.

It might come as a surprise (it did to us) that Oracle's Linux was announced in October 2006, and as we've mentioned, it was bred from Red Hat stock like some of the other flavours we've mentioned here. It was no surprise that Oracle decided to release its own Linux. Since the performance of an application is directly influenced and impacted by the performance of the underlying operating system, why not take the operating system – for which the source code is freely available – and make your own flavour that you can lace with the fruits from the knowledge of the application developers?

Hot Tip

There are more Linux distros than you can shake a stick at. Of the ones we haven't concentrated on Mint is one of the most popular, so take a look.

Below: Oracle Linux is based on Red Hat and has been operational since 2006.

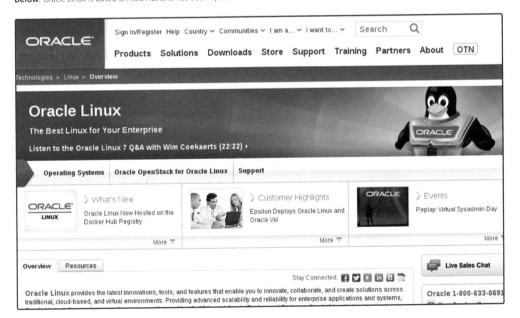

'Have there been no new Linuxes since 2006?' we hear you ask. And yes, absolutely, there have been – the likes of Evolve OS (renamed Solus not so long ago), or SparkyLinux. There are plenty of others that have been around a while too – Linux Mint is hugely popular since its arrival in 2006. Any Linux book can only ever scratch the surface of this market full of products.

WHAT DO ALL THE DISTROS HAVE IN COMMON?

There's a load of commonality to all the distros, which is why it can often be difficult to choose between them.

At the bottom, they all have a Linux kernel, though the versions vary. Generally speaking, the open source versions are slightly ahead of the commercial ones, since the commercial ones have to undergo more formal testing and need to be more supportable (which means bleeding-edge versions are avoided). So RHEL 7.1 has kernel 3.10, and back in the free world, so does CentOS 7.1 (remember we mentioned the two keep in step earlier?). Fedora 22, on the other hand, has kernel 4.0.

Accessing File Systems

Linuxes also have the ability to access file systems – segments of computers' onboard hard disks. There are file system formats that Linux considers 'native' (that is, you'd use them as the format for a disk holding Linux executables and data files), and they're called things like ext4 and reiserFS. Most Linuxes are also able to read – and usually, but not always, write – non-native file systems, the most obvious being the FAT and FAT32 file systems used by many Windows releases over the years and the NTFS format used by the more recent Windows incarnations. NTFS has historically been tricky with Linux – read-only access was the order of the day, and we've killed Windows partitions before by trying to write them using experimental NTFS drivers – but these days, you're OK.

Vital Core Abilities

Network support is also common: even the tiniest Linux machine will usually need to talk to something via a network, whether it's wireless or cabled. And similarly, core is the ability to drive a screen of some sort so you can boot the thing and see what it's doing. Finally, you'll generally have some kind of keyboard connectivity, with USB being the order of the day.

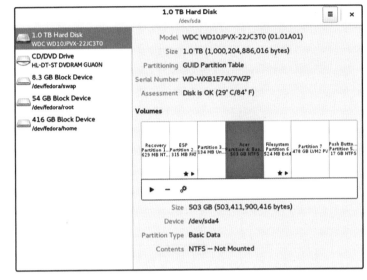

Above: A dual-boot hard disk is shown here; the blue segment is the Windows partition with the rest as Linux.

Hot Tip

If you dual-boot Linux and Windows, check out the NTFS support on the distro you're planning to use. Some still only support it as read-only, which limits the usefulness.

WHERE ARE THE DIFFERENCES?

The differences between Linuxes tend to come in two flavours, the first of which is the default setup of the product. That is, you'll sometimes find that although two Linux versions have support for pretty much the same processors, disk interfaces, graphics cards, network adaptors and so on, the default setups will vary slightly.

So for instance, if you install CentOS and pick the default options, you'll find it wants to format the disks in xfs format and give you the Gnome window manager by default. Fedora's also a Gnome lover, but our test machine tells us that it decided to use ext4 format for its disks. RHEL is xfs and Gnome (very CentOS again) and SUSE is presently using ext3 and Gnome.

Do the differences matter? In some cases, not enormously; as far as the user is concerned an ext3 disk behaves pretty much like an ext4 one or an xfs one – unless you're talking about absolutely massive file systems or really busy disks – and if you're installing in an environment like that, then you'll be reading the vendor's recommendations on the options that fit you best. Remember that we're just talking the default file system; you can generally hit the 'Customize' button and pick another if you wish.

Below: The Gnome desktop help page.

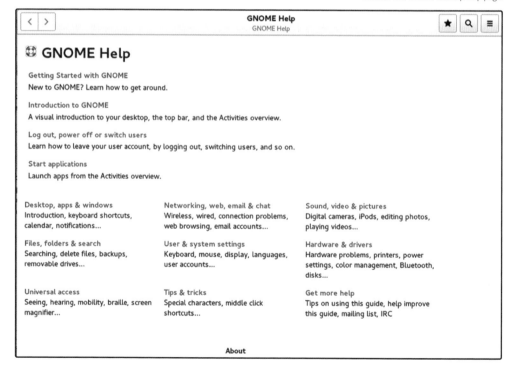

Changes to the System

In other cases, the differences are more relevant because they directly affect how you use the system. Different window managers will put things in different places on the screen, so switching between multiple environments can challenge your sanity if you have three machines running three different window managers that all have bits of the GUI in different places, or have interactive help screens that differ in quality and usability. Window managers are easy to replace, although the package groups can be hundreds of megabytes, so make sure you're not short on disk space.

Different Package Managers

The most confusing difference with distros is where they have different package managers. The Fedora installation we used in our examples uses DNF, which is a successor of the Yum package manager. Red Hat uses RPM. Yum and DNF both work with RPM packages, so are largely the same (albeit with different syntax). Debian users will be used to the Advanced Packaging Tool (APT). They all do pretty much the same thing, except that DNF is a modern alternative of Yum and they have different syntaxes; it's just that if you have different flavours you'll need to remember the different commands.

SIZE

The other big difference you'll find with Linux distros is their size. While this sounds a little bizarre (surely Linux is Linux?), it makes sense: if everyone's requirements were the same, there wouldn't be a market for dozens and dozens of different Linux distros.

Index of /pub/linux/distributions/damnsmall/current/

Name	Size	Date Modified
[parent directory]		
1-readme_first.txt	720 B	2/9/06, 12:00:00 AM
bootfloppy-utils.img	1.4 MB	8/10/08, 12:00:00 AM
bootfloppy-utils.img.md5.txt	55 B	8/10/08, 12:00:00 AM
bootfloppy.img	1.4 MB	7/8/08, 12:00:00 AM
bootfloppy.img.md5.txt	49 B	7/8/08, 12:00:00 AM
current.iso	0 B	12/20/10, 12:00:00 AM
current.iso.md5.txt	46 B	11/17/08, 12:00:00 AM
documentation/		4/14/07, 12:00:00 AM
dsl-3.x/		8/13/08, 12:00:00 AM
dsl-4.4.10-embedded.zip	50.6 MB	11/17/08, 12:00:00 AM
dsl-4.4.10-embedded.zip.md5.txt	58 B	11/17/08, 12:00:00 AM
dsl-4.4.10-initrd.iso	50.2 MB	11/17/08, 12:00:00 AM
dsl-4.4.10-initrd.iso.md5.txt	56 B	11/17/08, 12:00:00 AM
dsl-4.4.10-syslinux.iso	50.0 MB	11/17/08, 12:00:00 AM
dsl-4.4.10-syslinux.iso.md5.txt	58 B	11/17/08, 12:00:00 AM
dsl-4.4.10-vmx.zip	49.3 MB	11/17/08, 12:00:00 AM
dsl-4.4.10-vmx.zip.md5.txt	53 B	11/17/08, 12:00:00 AM
dsl-4.4.10.iso	49.9 MB	11/17/08, 12:00:00 AM
dsl-4.4.10.iso.md5.txt	49 B	11/17/08, 12:00:00 AM
extra_modules/		3/26/08, 12:00:00 AM
frugal_lite.sh	2.0 kB	9/1/05, 12:00:00 AM
kernel/		11/2/07, 12:00:00 AM
pcmciafloppy.img	1.4 MB	10/24/07, 12:00:00 AM
pcmciafloppy.img.md5.txt	51 B	10/24/07, 12:00:00 AM
pdfdocs/		4/14/07, 12:00:00 AM

Above: Damn Small Linux is a functional distro, despite its size.

So the mainstream Linux distros we've mainly discussed here are what you'd call general purpose: they take a few hundred megabytes or a few gigabytes on your hard disk, which is fine because you probably have a decent processor and a few hundred gigabytes of hard-disk space. But what if you're limited? Take the hugely popular Raspberry Pi, which started life with 256MB of onboard memory and relied on an SD card for its disk storage in the days when 16GB was considered quite big for an SD card. One of the references we used when researching this section had the onboard memory requirement for a basic installation of anywhere between 16MB (no surprise that this was for the Damn Small Linux distro) and 1GB (for the likes of Fedora).

PROCESSOR PLATFORM

Last, and by no means least, we have processor support as the key differentiator between distros. If you're based on Intel-style processors (x86 or x86-64), then you're spoilt for choice – though don't for a moment think that all Linuxes support these processors, as Yellow Dog users with their PowerPC-based Macs will attest. Of the non-Intel-style processors, the ARM range is supported by a decent range of distros, and as well as Yellow Dog, those PowerPC friends of ours also have a fair range of options. Beyond these, you're into pretty specialist processor architectures. You can run Debian or Fedora on your IBM s390x processor, for example, or if you have a MIPS architecture, your choices include Debian and Parabola. Why do you care? Well, if you have a multi-platform installation that you want to modify, there's something to be said for running different flavours of the same distro on the variety of kit.

Gentoo Linux

There's one distro we've not touched on yet, incidentally, and that's because it's bonkers and deserves a special mention all of its own. We just checked the download page for Gentoo Linux and it gave us the choice of x86, x86-64, Alpha, ARM, HPPA, IA-64, PowerPC, s390, SuperH and SPARC. Oh, and a MIPS version that's labelled 'experimental'. Linux distros don't get any more cross-platform than that.

Hot Tip

You probably don't have an IBM mainframe in your shed, so one of the x86 or x86-64 ones will be good enough.

WHAT HARDWARE TO USE

If you're going to run Linux, you'll need something to run it on. For now, we'll assume that you're going to be using a real, live, physical computer of some description (Linux on Cloud services like Amazon Web Services is great, but not what we're here to talk about). The great thing with modern Linux implementations is that the range of hardware they support is vast – so you have a range of options, from PCs you've put together in your shed up to high-performance commercial machines.

INTEL VERSUS OTHER PROCESSORS

Those of us who are old enough to remember will recall that Windows was once more than just an operating system for Intel processors. Windows NT was also available for the DEC Alpha processor, and in fact, we've seen it with our own eyes. Similarly, Sun's Solaris isn't just compatible with Sun's own SPARC processors, but also has x86 and x86-64 support (and, of course, its ancestors in the SunOS days supported the 68000-series processor family and the PowerPC processor was supported in one short-lived version).

Distribution	X86	X86-64	IA64	POWER	SPARC	ARM	MIPS	SH	IBM MAINFRAME	ALPHA
CentOS		Yes								
Debian	Yes	Yes		Yes		Yes	Yes			
Fedora	Yes	Yes				Yes				
Gentoo	Yes	Yes	Yes	Yes	Yes	Yes		Yes	Yes	Yes
openSUSE	Yes	Yes								
Oracle Linux	Yes	Yes	Yes							
Red Hat Enterprise Linux		Yes		Yes					Yes	
Slackware	Yes	Yes								
SUSE Linux Enterprise Server	Yes	Yes	Yes	Yes					Yes	
Ubuntu	Yes	Yes		Yes		Yes				
Yellow Dog Linux			Yes							

CPU Technology

One of the amazing facts about Linux though, is that it doesn't just support two or three processor families but a ridiculous list of CPU technology. Of course we start with the obvious x86 and x86-64 architectures, but also PowerPC (things like the IBM RS/6000) and IBM's Power processor. Then there's the ARM processor, which makes it a super choice for an embedded operating system if you're building a small ARM-based device and you want to run custom software on it. Going up the scale though, it also supports big systems such as IBM's S/390 and System z mainframe architectures.

Which Processor?

See the table above showing which distros support which processors. It includes the processors for which mainstream versions are available; for instance, Fedora has 'secondary' versions for the likes of MIPS, but they're not included as these versions aren't guaranteed to make the release at release time.

Factors to Consider

The thing is, you won't decide you want to use Linux and then go on to decide on the platform you want to run it on. The choice of a hardware platform or an operating system is seldom an isolated decision, instead you select them as a pair.

Let's take an example. Say you're a corporate looking to run a large database system and you've decided that Oracle is the database package you want to use. You have a variety of choices: you could use Sun SPARC kit (which is of course now Oracle-owned) running Solaris, or you could use Intel-based kit running Windows, or you could go for a favourite Intel-based server provider (HP, perhaps, or Dell) running Oracle Linux and sit Oracle's database on top.

Hot Tip

Unless you have a particular reason to use some other wacky architecture, we'd go with x86-64 as the platform of choice – it's popular and cheap. Don't bother with 32-bit x86 if you can help it.

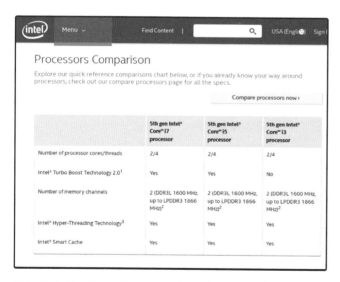

Above: It's best to pick a popular processor, unless you have very specific requirements.

SELF-BUILT DESKTOPS?

Those who build their own desktops tend to install Linux on them, for a simple reason – it's free. The alternative would be to install Microsoft Windows, but of course that's expensive. A few years ago we built a desktop machine for £254/$394; when you consider that a Windows licence is about £80/$124 on top of this, Linux is an attractive option. What do you need to consider when you're building your own machine?

Power

First there's the processor. We've discussed the different processor families, but here we're talking about building a PC so we're talking Intel or AMD processors. When it comes to the choice between a 32-bit and a 64-bit processor we always go 64-bit; the cost differential is negligible and as far as Linux is concerned there's absolutely no worry with it working as well on a 64-bit platform as it would on a 32-bit one.

Memory

Then we have on-board memory, and the answer is simple: as much as you can afford. Our lab laptop came with 8GB of RAM as standard, which is fine for what we need; if you're building a desktop why not start with 16Gb? The main rule we follow is to leave some RAM slots free for future expansion, so if you have four slots and you want 16GB use two 8GB modules instead of four 4GB ones.

Connection

Next is the network adaptor, and as you'll see shortly when we discuss networking, the only sensible option is Gigabit Ethernet. Motherboards come with on-board Gigabit Ethernet as standard.

While we're on motherboards, you'll find that the standard ones you can get will have SATA storage connections on-board; this is fine for a home-built desktop, and we'll explain a bit of what SATA is all about shortly in the section on storage, along with some advice on what disks to choose.

Other Bits of Kit

You'll also need a case and a power supply, but these are ten a penny. You can buy all kinds of funky cases for a home-build desktop, and all you need to remember is to decide how many internal hard disks you want and buy a case that's big enough to hold them.

Hot Tip

If you're self-building, get a motherboard/CPU package – it's so much easier than trying to comprehend which processor works with which motherboard.

The trickiest bit of building your own PC is matching the CPU with the motherboard – the spec sheets can be a bewildering series of socket types and such like. We tend to sidestep this by buying a kit that includes the motherboard and processor in a single box: you can get a kit for as little as about £160/$251, though, of course, the sky's the limit (£470/$739 for an Intel i5 on a motherboard with 8GB RAM, anyone?).

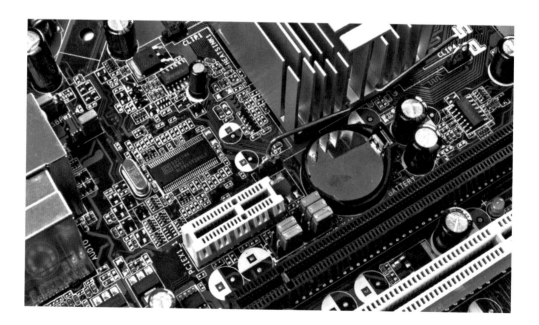

A SERVER IN YOUR COMPANY'S OFFICE

What do you do if you want a server for the office to run as a fileserver, or an email server, or a web server? Simple. Let's take an example of an entry-level, mainstream server – single processor, single 1TB hard disk and 8GB RAM. With Windows Server 2012, this comes in at £1,899/$2,988. Hang on though: if we decide to go for Red Hat Enterprise Linux, it actually goes up to £2,016/$3,172. And for SUSE, it's £2,102/$3,307.

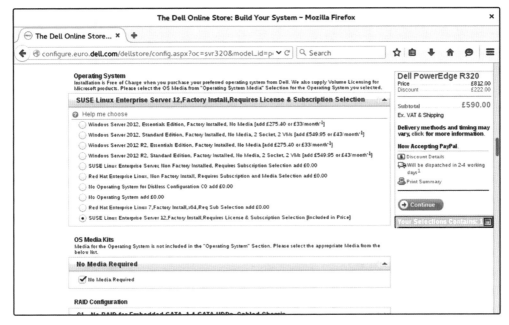

Above: Some vendors, such as Dell, now offer Linux with their new servers.

Makes Linux sound a little unattractive, then. But, of course, as we've said you don't have to use a commercial version of Linux if you're reasonably confident that you can look after the system yourself, or perhaps that you can engage a support partner to do it for you. Because if we check the price of the same server we just discussed with no installed operating system, the price of the box itself comes down to a mere £1,252/$1,969.

This isn't a big saving on a single box, but if you have two or three servers, it starts to add up. And this is our experience in small businesses – it starts with one or two machines and grows to perhaps four or five. The saving is tangible and can make a genuine difference. And even if you decide that you will go with at least some Windows servers (not a silly thing to do if you want to use native Active Directory support, for example), then there's nothing to stop you from integrating Linux servers into Active Directory so that the two platforms work in harmony.

Hot Tip

Linux support is more expensive than the commercial price of Windows, but you're getting more for your money in terms of live support from real technicians.

Comparing Costs

Remember that in comparing the Windows and Linux costs, you're not really comparing like for like; the commercial Linuxes give you not only the operating system and the ability to run updates, but also a variety of support such as helplines (Red Hat's standard support model gives you phone and web support for unlimited cases, for example). So although it's pricier, you get more for your money, even if you could have a self-serve option for free.

LINUX ON VIRTUAL MACHINES

As a final note in this section about running Linux in a small office, let's not forget the idea of virtual servers. This is where you use one or two fairly hefty physical servers and run a number of virtual servers – software-based servers that appear to everything on the network just like a physical machine but which share the resources of the physical kit they're sitting on. Virtualization is most definitely the order of the day even in many smallish companies, because it lets you separate functionality between separate virtual servers, whilst letting them share the hardware of the physical kit as efficiently as possible.

And, of course, every virtual server needs an operating system. If you spin up a Windows-based virtual server, then that'll cost you a Windows licence, but if you spin up a Linux one – specifically one of the free distros – then it won't cost an extra bean. Linux is brilliant for test, development and staging servers in a virtual setup, because you can run as many machines as you wish without spending any money.

WHAT TO CONNECT IT TO

When you're looking at the kit you're going to install Linux on, you also need to consider what you're connecting it to – the other devices on the network that you might want to use for file sharing, probably a printer and almost certainly an internet connection. We've talked about how to set up the network connectivity of Linux, but what about the network infrastructure itself?

Ethernet Networking

The first rule is that if you're using machines that aren't going to move very much (a Linux desktop, for instance), then use Ethernet networking – that is, use cables rather than wireless. WiFi is brilliant for portable devices, but if your device isn't portable, why not use a cable? Use Gigabit Ethernet: all new PC equipment will have a Gigabit port, and you can get a basic eight-port Gigabit network switch to connect it all to for about £20/$31, so there's no reason not to.

Wireless Networking

You're almost certain to use wireless networking for portable devices, of course, which may mean a Linux-based laptop. Make sure you turn on the best authentication and encryption options (WPA2 with AES encryption is the favourite), and make the shared key very cryptic so nobody can guess it. If you have a small number of devices, why not use your router's capability (and we bet it

has it) to assign a specific IP address to a specific machine based on the hardware address of its network adaptor? That means that if something's not working, you know what its IP address is meant to be, so you can try connectivity tests over the network.

Finally, wireless networks only really work properly through thin air – they don't like walls or doors. If you're going to have your Linux machines talking wirelessly to the rest of your kit, then make sure you go to the trouble of making the wireless network reliable, and use extender devices to improve the signal. There are two types of extender: the ones that are solely wireless (so they talk to your internet router wirelessly and then present themselves as a WiFi network) and the ones that use the mains power cabling to get the signal around the premises (so they're effectively cabled into the router and then presenting a WiFi network of their own). We use both, and performance is ten times better than we get if we power down all the extenders and let everything try to reach the central router.

Below: You can use a wireless extender to make sure your signal carries further.

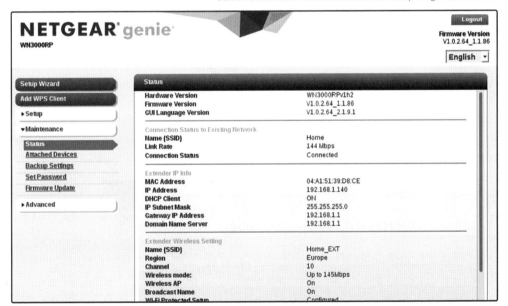

WHAT STORAGE TO USE

As we've mentioned, Linux will run on an enormous array of different hardware. One of the key things that influences its reliability though, is the storage you use to underpin the machine that it's running on. Computer storage is a vast subject, and the chances are that if you ask three people what storage they'd recommend for your Linux machine, you'll get at least two, if not three different answers. So here's an impartial view on what you should be doing.

TYPES OF DISK

The primary storage – the thing you'll boot your Linux system from – is the hard disk. These days, you have two options: 'traditional' magnetic disks (which we'll refer to as 'spinning disks') and Solid State Drives (otherwise known as SSD).

Spinning Disks

Spinning disks are just that – the storage unit is a set of disks coated with a magnetic material, which spin at high speed. A 'head' on a moving arm moves across the disks in order to write data on to the magnetic surface or to read it back off. An SSD, on the other hand, is made entirely of flash memory – there are no moving parts, but instead it uses solid-state memory that retains data when the device is off.

Above: The faster the spin speed of your spinning disk, the higher the price will be.

Spinning disks are available in different speed categories. Entry-level disks spin at 5,400 rpm, and at the high end, you're looking at 15,000 rpm. As you'd expect, the faster the spin speed, the faster the throughput of the disk – and the higher the price.

Solid State Drives

SSD is a whole different concept: it's considerably faster than spinning disk – so for instance, migrating from a spinning disk to an SSD unit can make your machine boot at least two or three times faster, and some specialist benchmark measurements have shown the difference to be way more than that. SSD is super-fast, and into the bargain you also get the fact that it's silent (there are no moving parts, as we mentioned) and the power consumption is lower than that of a spinning disk.

The other difference is the price. We just compared a 1TB SSD with a 1TB 5,400 rpm on a popular online retailer and the SSD was over five times the price (£254/$401 versus £46/$72). This reflects the fact that SSD is still a relatively new technology. Prices have already plummeted from where they were in the early days, and they continue to do so as the technology becomes cheaper to manufacture and the vendors compete.

Hot Tip

SSD used to be ridiculously expensive, but now it's merely very expensive! Prices are plummeting as it becomes popular, so check online stores for bargains.

Above: Solid State Drives use flash memory and have no moving parts.

INTERFACES

What also matters in terms of the storage you're using is the interface on the disks. If you're a corporate IT person building a big server installation, then you'll use Fibre Channel or Serial Attached Storage (known as SAS). These are high-speed interfaces and if you're using SSD, then it's absolutely essential for milking all the performance out of the expensive disks.

If you're a normal mortal putting together a desktop or laptop machine or a small server to do, say, your web development on, then you're more likely to choose a Serial ATA (known as SATA) interface. Disks with SATA interfaces tend to be cheaper than SAS or Fibre Channel but, more importantly, most desktop and laptop machines tend to have SATA disk interfaces by default, these days.

RESILIENCE

If you're building a Linux laptop then you'll usually have the ability to have a single internal disk in the machine. But if you're putting a desktop system together, there's usually the space to put more than one disk into the system. And this gives you a load more options when it comes to making your Linux machine more robust.

RAID

Storage technology has a concept called RAID, which originally stood for Redundant Array of Inexpensive Disks. These days, it's considered to mean Redundant Array of Independent Disks, because there's absolutely no necessity for the disks you use in a RAID array to be cheap and nasty – RAID works just as well with high-speed storage as with something inexpensive and pedestrian.

There are various configurations you can use for RAID, but the one we care about is RAID 1. With this approach, you have two disks connected to the adaptor card, and each item of data is written to both disks simultaneously. If one disk dies, the other just keeps on humming and the operation of your computer is unaffected as far as the user is concerned. There are other flavours of RAID, but for the average small or medium installation, you'll go for either RAID 1 or RAID 5 (in the latter, you have three disks and data is spread such that you can lose one with no effect).

The good news is that RAID is ridiculously inexpensive to build into a desktop machine – the retailer will want about £50 for a four-port 6Gbit/sec SATA RAID adaptor. Oh, and if you're thinking of using a software alternative to implement RAID without an adaptor – which Linux can do should you so wish – don't bother. The hardware is so cheap that you may as well hive that function off to an adaptor that specializes in it.

So if you're building a desktop machine, you'll want to look at your options – and the way to go is directly proportional to your budget! You have a few options open to you.

Below: MegaRAID adaptors list Linux in the supported operating systems.

Avago TECHNOLOGIES | STORAGE BY LSI™

Product Brief

MegaRAID® SAS 9380-8e
High Performance 12Gb/s PCI Express SATA+SAS RAID Controller
for External Storage Enclosures

Key Features

- High performance 12Gb/s data transfer rates
- Eight external 12Gb/s SATA+SAS ports
- Two mini-SAS SFF8644 external connectors
- LSI SAS 3108: 1.2GHz PowerPC® 476 dual core 12Gb/s ROC
- PCI Express 3.0 host interface
- 1GB DDRIII cache memory
- RAID levels 0, 1, 5, 6, 10, 50, and 60
- Support for CacheVault flash cache protection

Key Advantages

Outstanding RAID Performance for Next-Generation Servers and Storage

The explosive growth of data in cloud and enterprise data centers is driving the need for a higher performance storage interface to speed the ability of critical applications to access data. Avago Technologies first-to-market 12Gb/s SAS solutions are designed to deliver the performance and data protection capabilities required for the most demanding next-generation server and storage platforms. Offering up to double the data transfer rate of 6Gb/s SAS solutions, 12Gb/s SAS allows the SAS infrastructure to deliver bandwidth that can fully utilize that of PCI Express® 3.0 with a single controller card. The MegaRAID SAS 9380-8e, with eight external ports, delivers two 1.2GHz PowerPC® processor cores and a 72-bit DDRIII interface that drives 1GB cache memory. Powered by the LSI SAS 3108 dual-core ROC, the 9380-8e controller includes the latest PCI Express 3.0 and 12Gb/s SAS technology and is designed for configuring external storage enclosures with high-performance SAS hard drives, high-capacity SATA hard drives or application-accelerating solid state drives (SSDs).

JUST THE SINGLE DISK

If you're going for a single disk, get an SSD if you can afford it. The performance improvement will be vast when compared with the speed of a 'traditional' magnetic device, and as programs get bigger and slower (as seems to be the case over the last few years), you'll thank yourself for making the investment.

This also applies if you have a laptop. If you're restricted to having a single one, then why not make it a good one? The test machine we've been using for our examples here is clearly not the fastest in the universe, and you can tell when it's hammering the disk for a heavy chunk of access; it's definitely destined for an upgrade to SSD sooner rather than later.

SEPARATE BOOT DISK AND DATA DISK

Although you often hear people saying how fast their machine boots, does this really matter? If it's a laptop, then it probably does, as you'll tend to start up and shut down a lot. If it's a desktop, on the other hand, then perhaps not; our desktop iMac stays on most of the time – we seldom shut it down as it sits silently in the corner.

What you do care about is how fast it runs programs and accesses data. So if you want to optimize operating speed, why not have a small spinning disk as the boot disk but then install a larger SSD disk and use it for programs and data?

Once the kernel is in memory, it doesn't need to do any major access of the disk it booted from, so performance really isn't a big deal.

Hot Tip

Spend money on the data disk that's going to be accessed frequently, not the boot disk that only does anything when starting up.

```
                                    root@linuxpc-local:~

File  Edit  View  Search  Terminal  Help
[root@linuxpc-local ~]# smartctl  --all /dev/sda
smartctl 6.4 2015-06-04 r4109 [x86_64-linux-4.0.4-301.fc22.x86_64] (local build)
Copyright (C) 2002-15, Bruce Allen, Christian Franke, www.smartmontools.org

=== START OF INFORMATION SECTION ===
Model Family:     Western Digital Blue Mobile
Device Model:     WDC WD10JPVX-22JC3T0
Serial Number:    WD-WXB1E74X7WZP
LU WWN Device Id: 5 0014ee 6afbaad8e
Firmware Version: 01.01A01
User Capacity:    1,000,204,886,016 bytes [1.00 TB]
Sector Sizes:     512 bytes logical, 4096 bytes physical
Rotation Rate:    5400 rpm
Device is:        In smartctl database [for details use: -P show]
ATA Version is:   ACS-2 (minor revision not indicated)
SATA Version is:  SATA 3.0, 6.0 Gb/s (current: 6.0 Gb/s)
Local Time is:    Mon Aug 17 21:33:27 2015 BST
SMART support is: Available - device has SMART capability.
SMART support is: Enabled

=== START OF READ SMART DATA SECTION ===
SMART overall-health self-assessment test result: PASSED

General SMART Values:
Offline data collection status:  (0x00) Offline data collection activity
                                        was never started.
```

Above: Smartctl lets you dig into the detail of your disks.

RAIDED DATA DISK

We've discussed the concept of backups (see page 107), and as you'll know if you've read that bit, it's often simpler to reinstall the operating system than to try to fix weird problems with it. Hence we've said that the main thing to concentrate on backing up is your data, as you can't reinstall that from a standard image. So why not RAID it?

What RAID offers, as we've said, is the ability for a disk to die without service being interrupted. You do, however, need to be a bit cautious when you pick your RAID adaptor, because you need to know when a disk has gone 'pop'. We're not going to suggest specific controller cards, because the choice varies with budget and there's every chance that some of them will have been superseded between us typing this and you reading it. The trick is to find some candidate devices, then study the spec sheets carefully (and ask Google) to verify that either there's a Linux version of the management utility or that standard Linux commands such as smartctl can interrogate it. The usual guidance is to stick with mainstream vendors like Adaptec or LSI, as support is generally better for the better-known vendors.

REPLACING DISKS

Most RAID adaptors allow you to use different disks yet still run a RAID 1 setup. Now, you wouldn't do this for fun – if you're building a new PC, then you'll buy a RAID adaptor and two identical disks, of course. But if one of the disks fails, there's every chance you won't be able to purchase an identical model – disks become obsolete and new models appear in their place all the time. Generally though, as long as you replace it with one that's (a) as fast as the broken one and (b) at least as big as the failed unit, the adaptor will generally be able to cope. Of course, you won't be able to use the whole space of the disk, but that's the price you pay for resilience.

JUST BECAUSE IT KEEPS GOING

One final note on the subject of RAID adaptors: just because they can survive the death of an attached disk, this doesn't mean you can replace that disk without shutting down the server. The expensive RAID controllers in corporate servers do have 'hot swap' capability, where you leave the server running while you pull out the failed device and push in a new one. The inexpensive devices for small servers and desktops don't have hot-swap features, so you'll often find that in order to swap the disks, you have to power down the box and change the components. Of course, you at least have the freedom to choose a time when the system's not being used to power it down, and if you're handy with a screwdriver, it shouldn't take more than 15–20 minutes to swap out a disk before powering up again.

HOW DOES IT REBUILD?

When you replace a failed disk, the controller takes on the task of duplicating the data from the working one to the blank replacement. This is an automatic process, but it's often not a fast one – it can take a few hours before the two are in synch and the system is fully resilient again. If you've been diligent and chosen your adaptor wisely, you'll be able to check on the status of the disk and see when it's back to a resilient state.

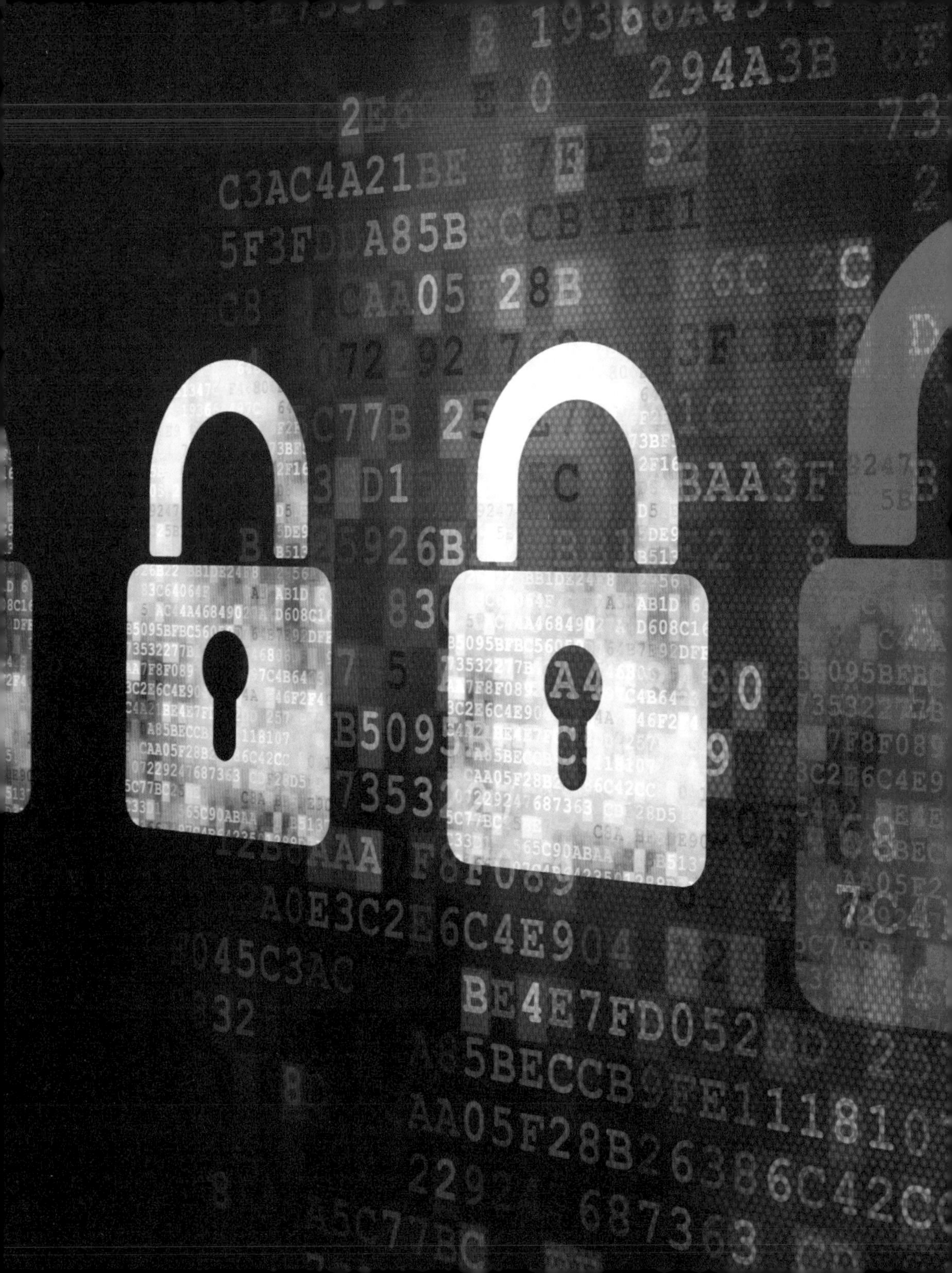

LINUX AND SECURITY

STAYING SAFE ONLINE

Linux has a reputation for being an incredibly secure operating system. But what makes it so? What does Linux have that, say, Windows or MacOS doesn't? Particularly given that MacOS is a flavour of Unix not unlike Linux anyway.

Well, first is the basic security model. Where operating systems such as the Windows family allow you to provide a given user ID with permissions ranging from nothing to everything (including whatever variant you wish in between), Linux doesn't. You're either the super-user ('root') or you're not, and no matter what wacky permissions you give people, they simply can't do high-privilege actions unless they become root. Secondly, the writers of malware and viruses tend to concentrate on the more popular platforms (primarily Windows), because the more popular the platform, the more likely they're going to be to infect someone's system.

Don't think for a moment though, that Linux can't be made insecure – because it can. It's a powerful operating system and as such it's perfectly possible to configure it so that, for example, a normal user can execute a program as root. But you have to be (a) the root user in order to do this, as well as, (b) a bit naïve. Similarly, there have been virus-like malware programs for Unix-style operating systems over the years too – even back as far as 1988, when the 'Morris worm' became the first internet virus when it exploited security vulnerabilities in some Unix implementations.

KEEPING LINUX SECURE

But although Linux can be made insecure, it's generally very secure – so let's talk about why that is and how you can keep it that way. There are two sides to security: making sure your machine isn't available for people to connect randomly into and wander about in your files; and being sensible about what you do online.

NAT AND THE NETWORK YOUR MACHINE SITS ON

The chances are that your Linux machine is sitting on a home or small office network, and that it's accessing the internet in the same way as, say, Windows PCs, tablet computers and smartphones. This generally means that you have a router that allocates your computer an IP address and performs what's called Network Address Translation (NAT) when you want to browse to a website out there in the big wide world.

Hot Tip

The average home or small office network has NAT even if you didn't realize it. It's well worth understanding, as it helps comprehend how your network works at all.

Private IP Addresses

To understand NAT, you need to understand the concept of a private IP address. And to be honest, the clue is in the word 'private'. The internet has a concept called a Request For Comments (RFC), which is a badly chosen name because the various documents are regarded pretty much as standards even if they're not labelled as such. Now, RFC1918 (check out https://tools.ietf.org/html/rfc1918 for the official text) is called Address Allocation for Private Internets, and it tells us that there are some address ranges that are considered private:

- ● 10.0.0.0 – 10.255.255.255
- ● 172.16.0.0 – 172.31.255.255
- ● 192.168.0.0 – 192.168.255.255

Outbound Connections

The trick with private IP addresses is that the routers owned by your ISP won't route traffic to or from these addresses, which means that nobody can make a connection from the internet into your Linux machine if it has one of these addresses.

Above: Network control panel showing IP addresses.

The trouble is, of course, that this will also stop you making outbound connections, because the internet won't know how to route the reply back to your machine. This is where NAT comes in, because what happens is:

- ● The PC, with its private address, makes an outbound connection, which lands at the router.

- ● The router, whose internet port has a public IP address that the internet *can* route to, takes note of the connection from a PC and does some funky translation so the remote server sees the connection as coming from the router's public address.

○ The response comes back to the router on its public IP address.

○ The router reverses the funky translation and passes the response to the PC.

Now, although devices on the internet can see the router's public address and can try to send it data, it'll only accept things that it knows are the replies to the requests it sent out. Hence your PC is implicitly protected against random attacks from the internet.

Hot Tip

Always use private addresses internally. It's the standard for all routers anyway, and it means you can be sure nobody can route directly to your machine from the internet.

Username:	ddgetss34
Password:	••••••••
MRU:	1492
Maxfail:	0
Keepalive retry:	10
Keepalive interval:	60

☐ Proxy ARP
☑ Persist
☐ On demand
    Idle time: 60
☐ Debug

Firewall

☑ Firewall
☑ NAT
☑ Clamp TCP MSS to path MTU
DMZ host IP address: 192.168.1.186

Default routing

Confirmation: ◉ None
  ◯ Required for HTTP traffic
  ◯ Required for all traffic

Apply   Reset   Delete

Above: The page on a Tilgin home router, on which you can set up a DMZ host IP address.

Hot Tip

Don't use a DMZ host to permit inbound connections unless you're absolutely happy about what it means – and unless you've turned off all nonessential services and tightened up your firewall.

DMZ HOSTS

Now, there's a modest possibility that you might actually want to permit some kind of inbound connections from the internet. Maybe you run a little web server in your garage, for example. Most home routers allow you to permit some basic incoming connections – usually by letting you set a DMZ (Demilitarized Zone) computer. It sounds a bit weird, but you basically tell the router: 'If you receive any inbound connections that don't correspond to outbound connections you know about, pass them to this internal address', where the internal address is the IP address of your Linux machine. Below is an example of how a Tilgin home router does it. We would put our Linux machine's IP address in the 'DMZ host IP address' box. If you're thinking of doing this, you'll want to read the firewall section later on (see pages 168–73).

OFF BY DEFAULT

As we saw when we were discussing things like making remote connections and running up a web server, most network services on a Linux machine are turned off by default. To make it listen for any network connections, we usually have to turn on the appropriate services first, otherwise incoming connections will simply be ignored. Always, always adopt this approach – if you don't need something to be listening on the network, turn it off.

For applications that you can't control through the user interface, make sure that you don't just stop the application but that you also disable it from coming back to life when you restart the

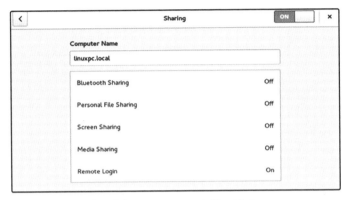

Above: Sharing control panel, showing services turned off by default.

machine. On Fedora, that means using `systemctl stop` to shut it down and `systemctl disable` to prevent it restarting when you reboot.

If you really want to be secure about things, and if you don't need a particular application that can accept network connections, then you ought to uninstall it rather than simply turning it off. The package manager can uninstall stuff for you as easily as it helped you install it.

Above: On Fedora, you can use `systemctl stop` and `systemctl disable`; alternatively, you can uninstall the application.

BE SENSIBLE WITH OUTBOUND CONNECTIONS

We've mentioned already that you can't seriously break Linux if you're a normal user without super-user root privileges. We did also mention though, that you can be a nuisance to others even if you're a normally privileged user. Say you're using one of the many free GUI-based email programs to read your mail on your Linux desktop. What would happen then if someone emailed you an attachment that was actually a script containing shell commands, which would send a bazillion emails to various addresses? Would you

Hot Tip

Linux is inherently secure, but if you do something daft such as running a script that someone has emailed to you, you're asking for trouble.

double-click it? Even if you just answered 'no', not everyone thinks the same. After all, we've all seen people who have double-clicked dodgy attachments on their Windows email program and infected their machine with a virus of some kind.

Be sensible, then. Just as you would with any other platform, think before you click, because although there aren't many Linux viruses, that doesn't mean there aren't any at all.

KEEP YOUR APPLICATIONS UPDATED

Finally, just as you would with any other platform, make sure you regularly update your applications and other Linux components. We've mentioned that you shouldn't just run a blanket update at every opportunity, as it runs the risk of breaking something, but similarly, you do need to ensure that everything is running at a reasonably recent version. The reason is simple: many Linux attacks rely on vulnerabilities (that is, bugs

with security implications) in the applications and other modules that run on the platform. So if you ensure you update things frequently, you can minimize the chance of someone exploiting an old, buggy version of something on your machine.

CONNECTING SAFELY

When Unix computers first became popular, it was common to use console terminals that connected directly to a serial (RS-232) port in the back of the system.

This was a nice, secure way to connect, because you had the physical security of the building and the room in which the terminals resided to control who could get at them. You also had the concept of a console, which was a special terminal (known as a 'secure' terminal). You could only log in as root on the console, and on standard terminals, you had to log in as a normally privileged user and then become the root user.

LOCAL AREA NETWORKS

This approach was very expensive: you needed multi-port serial adaptors in the back of the Unix machine and a serial cable running to each location where there was a terminal. It was inconvenient too: you could only connect from wherever there was a terminal. So the alternative – connecting over a Local Area Network (LAN) – became attractive.

TELNET

Telnet was the protocol that allowed many dozens of users to connect into a single Unix host via a LAN – generally, though not necessarily, Ethernet. A simple program on a client PC or Mac could very easily connect to the Unix machine and run a command line shell session in just the same way as a terminal did (and in fact, it was generally faster, since serial terminals were restricted to 2,400 or 9,600 bits per second, while the LAN ran at 10Mbit/s or more).

The problem with Telnet is that (a) it runs over a network connection that's shared with loads of other people and computers, and (b) everything you type or receive is transmitted in plain text – even your password and other potentially confidential information. It's not a difficult job to put a 'sniffer' on a network segment and watch the traffic as it flies past. So encryption is the order of the day.

Hot Tip

Never, ever use the Telnet server application. SSH is more secure and is absolutely standard these days, so there's no need even to consider its plain-text ancestor.

SSH

SSH is the Secure SHell (one of the many abbreviations with dodgy capitalization). The idea is simple: when the client computer connects to the server's SSH service, the two endpoints negotiate with each other to set up an encrypted communication channel, and once this has been established, the whole end-to-end process looks to the user just like a Telnet connection. The difference, however, is that anyone watching the traffic flying past by 'sniffing' the network will be disappointed, as all they'll see is a bunch of incomprehensible garbage that cannot easily be decoded by anyone other than one of the two endpoints legitimately involved in the interaction.

Careful of Complacency

When we say 'cannot easily be decoded', that's not to say SSH is entirely unbreakable. Time marches on and computers get more powerful, but in the general the task of breaking an SSH stream's encoding is *intractable*, which means it would take too long and take too much resource to warrant the effort.

Note also that while you generally authenticated on a traditional Telnet connection using a simple username/password exchange, these days you have various other tools at your disposal. So although you can still use a username/password combination, you also have the option of lodging digital certificates on the client and server. The benefit here is that from the first moment of connection, the two endpoints know the encryption mechanism and the key to use, and the credentials provided by a certificate are way more complex than a password. You've also got the option of using a one-time code or other two-factor authentication mechanism.

PUBLIC KEY ENCRYPTION IS BONKERS

While we're on the subject, we'll mention Public Key Encryption (PKE) – a technique that's used by SSH as well as other similar concepts such as the secure web protocol. When you use a digital certificate to encrypt or 'sign' a chunk of data, it has two 'keys' – a public one and a private one – which are mathematically related. When you set up a certificate, you keep the private key secret (again, the clues are there) and then you advertise to the world what the public key is. The cool thing with PKE is that if you encode something with someone's public key, they can very easily decode it with their private key, but the nature of the algorithm (the actual function used to do the encryption) is very hard to do in reverse. For this reason, it's often called a 'trapdoor algorithm' – if you only know the public key, it's very easy to go one way (encryption), but you'll struggle to go the other (decryption).

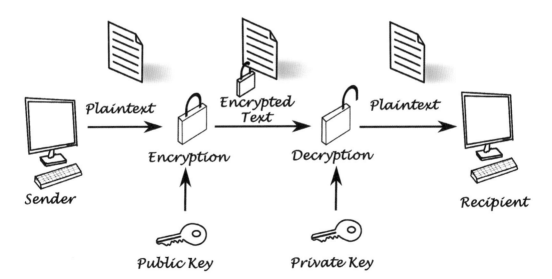

We're not about to describe how to do a PKE algorithm here, as it's more suited to an entire chapter than a small paragraph. It's also a completely bonkers idea, particularly because when you read about it (check out the RSA algorithm, the first mainstream PKE mechanism), you'll find yourself thinking: 'How on earth did they think of that?'

The main thing to remember about PKE is that as computers get faster, you need longer and longer keys in order to make it as hard as possible for someone to decrypt your transmissions. The longer the key, the more processor overhead you use to do the actual encryption.

Hot Tip

Read up on PKE. There's loads of material on the internet and although it can be heavy going, it's great when you've had the lightbulb moment and you feel you have a basic understanding.

Hot Tip

You may have to enable the SSHD application before some other programs will work, because they rely on an SSH channel being available before they can do their work.

SSH IS THE PATH TO OTHER FUNKY STUFF

The final thing to know about SSH is that it's not just a replacement for Telnet – it's usable for far more than text-based command-line sessions to remote computers. The IT world has a tendency to reuse technology instead of reinventing the wheel, and so you find other concepts piggy-backing on to SSH.

Take the File Transfer Protocol (FTP), for instance. This is another age-old internet standard and in its basic form, it sends data in unencrypted streams. It wasn't much of a leap of logic to say: 'Hang about, let's fire up an SSH connection and then do our FTP transfers through that.'

It made perfect sense to let the SSH software do the hard work of encryption and then simply throw the FTP traffic through the secure 'tunnel'. FTP is not alone – developers around the world use SSH as the underlying security layer for their proprietary protocols, because it's a dead easy way of achieving highly secure communication with no effort.

LINUX FIREWALLS

So far, we've talked a lot about Linux's inherent security in the sense that it doesn't listen for inbound network connections unless you tell it to, and that you can't break the core components unless you're the root user. But what about its firewall capability? Linux can not just refuse traffic because something happens not to be listening for it, but detect inbound traffic and actively decide whether it should be allowed in.

IPTABLES

We've mentioned IPTables, which is the most common Linux firewall package, because we've had to tweak its rules in order to make things work in our examples. If you think of the components of your Linux machine like an onion, you have the kernel at the core, with the applications in the

next layer and IPTables in the layer on top of that. If a connection doesn't get through IPTables, it's never going to reach the application, whether the latter is sitting listening or not.

PACKET FILTERING

The core functionality of IPTables is what's called packet filtering. The idea is simple: it analyses every packet (a 'packet' is the basic unit of data on a network) and decides what to do with it based on what it sees. Decisions can be made based on the various aspects of the packet content – for instance:

- If a packet comes in from another machine destined for our Linux machine with a destination port of 80 (the standard web server port), and we know we don't want to run a web server, drop that packet.

- If our Linux machine tries to send a packet out to another machine with a destination port of 23 (the standard Telnet port), we could tell IPTables to drop it because we don't want our local users using the insecure Telnet protocol.

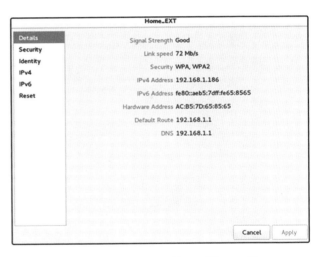

Hot Tip

Like many things with Linux, IPTables rulesets can look scary. But just work through them one by one and you'll get it – everything's logical, just a bit cryptic-looking.

Above: Interface configuration showing IP address and Ethernet address.

- If we've detected an unknown device on our network with a particular Ethernet adaptor address (perhaps one of our machines is alerting us that there's a machine with that Ethernet address spraying our network with junk), we could tell IPTables to drop packets to and from that device.

IPTABLES RULE CATEGORIES

When you're configuring IPTables to secure the machine it sits on, there are two categories of rule (they're called 'chains' in IPTables parlance) we're particularly interested in.

One-way Traffic

First, we have the input chain, and as you might guess, this chain is all about traffic that comes into our machine from anywhere else. You've seen that the various examples scattered around this book have the input chain mentioned in the commands we've executed – it's all about connections that originate elsewhere and land on us.

The Other Way

In the opposite direction, we have the output chain, and it'll be no surprise that this is all about connections that originate on our machine and are destined for elsewhere. Why do we care about these? Simple: if someone manages to exploit a bug in one of the programs on our Linux machine (or, more likely, the user double-clicks a malicious attachment in an email

```
                                        iptables [Read-Only]
 Open  ▾    ᒪᑎ                             /etc/sysconfig                        Save   ≡   ✕
# Generated by iptables-save v1.4.21 on Sun Aug 16 16:50:45 2015
*nat
:PREROUTING ACCEPT [3631:1489246]
:INPUT ACCEPT [53:4443]
:OUTPUT ACCEPT [752:49166]
:POSTROUTING ACCEPT [752:49166]
:OUTPUT_direct - [0:0]
:POSTROUTING_ZONES - [0:0]
:POSTROUTING_ZONES_SOURCE - [0:0]
:POSTROUTING_direct - [0:0]
:POST_FedoraWorkstation - [0:0]
:POST_FedoraWorkstation_allow - [0:0]
:POST_FedoraWorkstation_deny - [0:0]
:POST_FedoraWorkstation_log - [0:0]
:PREROUTING_ZONES - [0:0]
:PREROUTING_ZONES_SOURCE - [0:0]
:PREROUTING_direct - [0:0]
:PRE_FedoraWorkstation - [0:0]
:PRE_FedoraWorkstation_allow - [0:0]
:PRE_FedoraWorkstation_deny - [0:0]
:PRE_FedoraWorkstation_log - [0:0]
-A PREROUTING -j PREROUTING_direct
-A PREROUTING -j PREROUTING_ZONES_SOURCE
-A PREROUTING -j PREROUTING_ZONES
-A OUTPUT -j OUTPUT_direct
-A POSTROUTING -j POSTROUTING_direct
-A POSTROUTING -j POSTROUTING_ZONES_SOURCE
-A POSTROUTING -j POSTROUTING_ZONES
-A POSTROUTING_ZONES -o wlp2s0 -g POST_FedoraWorkstation
-A POSTROUTING_ZONES -g POST_FedoraWorkstation
-A POST_FedoraWorkstation -j POST_FedoraWorkstation_log
-A POST_FedoraWorkstation -j POST_FedoraWorkstation_deny
                               Plain Text ▾   Tab Width: 8 ▾    Ln 1, Col 1    ▾    INS
```

Above: An example of an IPTables config file.

message) a strong filter in the output chain will prevent us becoming the source of loads of unwanted outbound connections to the machine of some unsuspecting victim.

The Third Way

There is a third chain, which becomes of interest when we're looking to use our IPTables-equipped Linux machine to do more than just secure its own connectivity. What if you want to put it at the edge of your network and use it to permit and deny traffic flows where the source and destination are both other machines? This is where the forward chain comes in. It works in the same way as input and output with regard to the decisions it can make, with the difference that it's for packets that neither start nor finish on the local machine. Oh, and if you're wondering whether IPTables can act as a NAT router to protect a network in the same way as our home router that we mentioned earlier ... then yes, absolutely. There are two more chains called prerouting and postrouting that you can use to do the NAT 'masquerading' – the IP address rewriting we described earlier.

SELINUX

Hand-in-hand with IPTables on today's Linux
machines is the SELinux (Security Enhanced Linux)
package. It's not an alternative to IPTables, but a
complementary package that's implemented as a
kernel module and which provides additional security
in a different way. So while IPTables is all about
defining whether network traffic gets in or out,
SELinux is more about which components within

Hot Tip

**SELinux is a bit harder to get
to grips with than IPTables, as
the documentation can be a
bit cryptic, but be persistent
and you'll be fine.**

our Linux machine are allowed to interact with each other, and to what extent. As the
SELinux production team puts it, it allows you 'to define how applications and users can
access different resources such as files, devices, networks and inter-process communication'.
SELinux is all about using 'policies' to restrict access only where it's required. However, the
motivation is the same as that of IPTables – specifically to prevent nefarious activity whilst
permitting the functionality we actually desire.

You'll remember
from our example
of setting Linux up
as a NAS that we
had to use the
'setsebool -P samba_
enable_home_ dirs
on' directive before
SELinux would let
us access Max's
home directory as
a shared folder.

Left: SELinux policy examples.

LINUX AS A FIREWALL?

So we've discussed how Linux can protect itself using both network-level security (IPTables) and internal restrictions about what can access what (SELinux). But would you actually use Linux as a firewall if you were, say, running a small business and you wanted to secure your world? To be honest, probably not. You certainly wouldn't decide to take your fileserver and configure IPTables as your corporate firewall too. Why would you turn your main data repository into something that you actively expect to have to fend off attacks? If your cheap router isn't up to the job, there are a number of dedicated devices on the market that will be a lot easier to set up and are probably a lot more reliable than having a PC with a spinning disk just waiting to die.

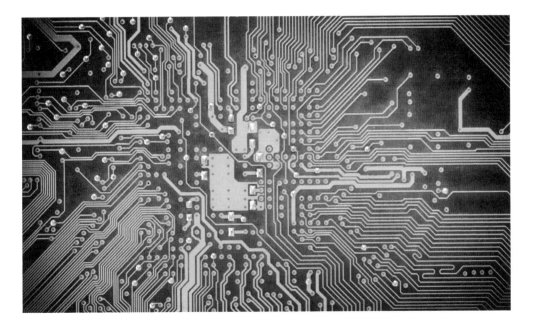

So use the tools available to you – IPTables and SELinux – to secure your Linux machines, but we wouldn't suggest you rush to use it as the security device for protecting your world, as there are far easier ways than that.

WIRELESS SECURITY

The last area of security in the world of Linux is wireless security. We've already touched briefly on the wireless networking options open to you, so now we'll have a proper look at them.

WHEN NOT TO USE WIRELESS

It's perhaps slightly odd in a chapter about wireless security to talk about why you wouldn't use it, but there are some perfectly good reasons why you would look to use cabled networking in certain situations.

Static Machines

If you have a desktop PC near a network outlet that you can connect easily to the network via a copper or fibre cable, just do it. While the inventors of wireless networking are trying their hardest to make their brainchild go faster and faster, they're still way behind the cable-based lot. Buy a desktop PC today and it'll come with a built-in Gigabit Ethernet port, and at the infrastructure end, the switching aspect is pretty cheap too.

Diagnosing Problems

Cabled networks are also far easier to diagnose than wireless ones, as you know precisely what's connected to what and can easily track down rogue traffic to specific devices or switch ports.

This said though, we all want to do more and more wireless networking – not least with our smartphones and tablets and those laptops (Linux-based ones, hopefully) that we love to cart around wherever we go. The MacBook Pro we're typing this on doesn't actually have an Ethernet port (to use a cabled connection requires a little dongle) and so wireless is increasingly becoming the order of the day.

Hot Tip

We've told you to use wired networking where you can, but if it's not feasible, then wireless is fine – and if you've used cables for some machines, it leaves the wireless network for sharing between fewer devices (which means it'll go faster).

THE WIRELESS INFRASTRUCTURE MATTERS

Wireless networking isn't trivial if you do it properly. As we sit writing this, we're connected not to the wireless router that drives our network, but to a small extender unit that's taking our data streams and throwing them at the router via the mains circuit of the building (this is a popular way of increasing your wireless coverage, incidentally, as it's fast and cheap). That's fine, as we've been careful to secure everything. Like most of you reading this, we can see several wireless networks in their 'available networks' list that are nothing to do with us and which are potentially causing interference in terms of radio channels.

Simple Security Measures

If you do use multiple devices to ensure that your wireless network is as available as possible in your building, try to use extenders that genuinely extend the network instead of acting as a shedload of different networks. Many of the offerings on the market these days let you do this, and it means you configure each PC once for a single network instead of having separate network IDs and encryption levels for each of the access devices on the premises.

Administration Interfaces

Make sure to secure your wireless devices' administration interfaces. Your router is probably also your wireless infrastructure, and most people have never changed the admin password on the device. We were at a pub quiz, and were impressed that they had a wireless system that used an iPad app for buzzing in. In the interval, once we'd logged into the wireless router's maintenance page (username 'admin', password 'password') it was very tempting to tell it to block connections from all quizzers but us. We're about to tell you to set a complex key for your wireless connection, so don't ruin it by forgetting to secure the router itself.

WIRELESS SECURITY PROTOCOLS

Let's have a quick recap of the various wireless security protocols. If you recall, they're split into two categories: authentication/admission control and encryption. Authentication first, then.

- **WEP (Wired Equivalent Privacy):** Prehistoric technology that you shouldn't touch with a bargepole. It was fine when it came about in the 1990s, but these days, it's easier to crack than an egg.

- **WPA (WiFi Protected Access):** Far better than WEP, but it has been superseded (as you'll see in a moment). If your wireless infrastructure is quite old, this might be the only non-WEP protocol available to you, but it's more likely that you'll have the option of ...

- **WPA2:** The new version of WPA. The best so far and the one to choose. If all your wireless devices are new enough to support WPA2, then switch your wireless infrastructure to use only WPA2 and permit no others. The main development of WPA2 is that it includes support for more secure encryption protocols than its predecessor.

Moving on to encryption, the options you get depends on your chosen authentication protocol. With WEP all of the security options are utterly appalling because it's so antiquated and hence the standard never reached the stage of having sufficiently complex encryption to cope with modern cracking methods. With the WPA family you get the option of the Temporal Key Integrity Protocol (TKIP) or the CCMP encryption standard. The latter is based on AES, or the Advanced Encryption Standard, and is considered the gold standard right now, so just use it and don't think about TKIP.

Remember, You're Not a Company

You're not running a corporate network, so if you see options such as 'WPA-Enterprise' when you're setting up your equipment, you can largely disregard them. This option lets you do clever things like installing a digital certificate on each of your portable devices and authenticating your phone, tablet or laptop against a corporate security server to verify that it's genuinely a device that belongs on the corporate network. It's very cool, but almost certainly not something you'll use if you're reading this book (at least not yet).

Above: Choose a very secure password for your wireless network.

PASSWORD PROTECTION

The way your device will authenticate, then, is a Pre-Shared Key (PSK). As it sounds, this is a string of characters that's configured into the wireless infrastructure and which you also enter into any device that wants to connect to the network. When the PC attempts to connect to the wireless network, it negotiates a connection then the two parties verify that the client machine has the right key. It should go without saying that you need to make your PSK as unguessable as possible and as long as is reasonable (it can be up to 63 characters). Ours is 21 characters long and contains a suitable collection of upper- and lower-case characters, digits and punctuation, but it's still sufficiently memorable that we don't make too many attempts when trying to remember it when we get yet another new tablet or smartphone.

ROGUE ACCESS POINTS

The last thing we'll talk about in our discussion of wireless network security is when you come across wireless stuff that's nothing to do with you. As we said earlier, it's perfectly normal when selecting a wireless network to see a bunch of names that you don't recognize. Although your own wireless signal can be frustratingly attenuated when it passes through the flimsiest of doors or stud walls, it sometimes feels like six inches of lead wouldn't keep next door's wireless network from being visible in your living room. That's not overly problematic if it's your neighbour's legitimate network (except when their kit decides to talk on the same channel as yours and kills the throughput). But what if someone's run up a nefarious wireless device with the same network name you're expecting to see and has allowed connectivity without requiring a key?

The answer is that you have to be cautious and sensible. Tell your machine that it's not allowed to connect to any old network, without you specifically selecting it, and when you're connecting to your legitimate network make sure it asks you for the PSK (if it doesn't, you've probably been nabbed by the dodgy network because yours should demand authentication).

KEEP ON TOP OF IT

Above all with wireless security, keep on top of developments. Happily, it's one of the areas of IT that doesn't change all that often. WPA2 has been with us since 2004, for example, and so there's no annual panic to get to grips with new standards. WPA2 is perfectly fine, and CCMP/AES is great for encryption, but don't ruin it by forgetting to change the admin password of the router and letting any old idiot get into the router config page.

Hot Tip

Be suspicious of any new network you see, and don't try to connect to it. There are malware programs that advertise themselves as WiFi networks, just waiting to pounce when you connect.

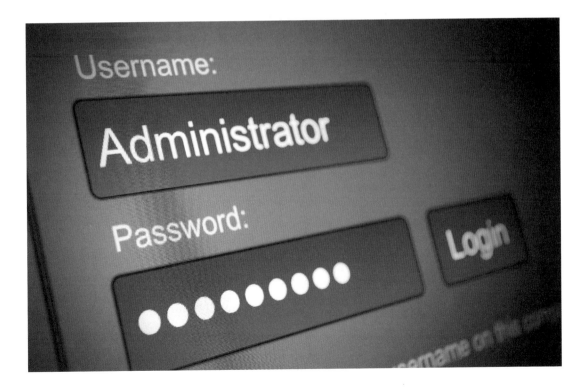

LINUX AND NETWORKING

GETTING CONNECTED

Computer networking has changed hugely over the years. The strange thing is though, that unlike pretty much everything else in the universe, the world of networking hasn't quadrupled in complexity. In fact, it's actually got simpler.

These days, the only network protocol the average computer user comes across is IP – the Internet Protocol. That wasn't the case until the late 1990s, before which we had an unbelievable range of network protocols. Just to pick a few, we had DECnet (from Digital Equipment Corporation, who invented it to let PDP-11 minicomputers talk to each other), AppleTalk (from Apple in the mid-1980s to hook Macs together via their built-in LocalTalk ports), IPX (another 1980s vintage protocol, this time from Novell and the default in their NetWare operating system)

and X.25 (hugely popular around the same time for wide area networks).

The underlying connectivity on top of which all these protocols sat has got simpler too. As well as the LocalTalk connection mechanism built into Macs, we also had IBM's Token Ring, FDDI (a fibre technology, which at 100Mbit/s was considered super-fast in its day), ATM (a telecoms technology that tried but failed to take off in data networking) and many others. Linux has always had support for an enormous range of network protocols – just some of them can be seen in the screenshot of the kernel configuration application. Nowadays, it's pretty much Ethernet across the board for cabled connections; we'll come to wireless shortly.

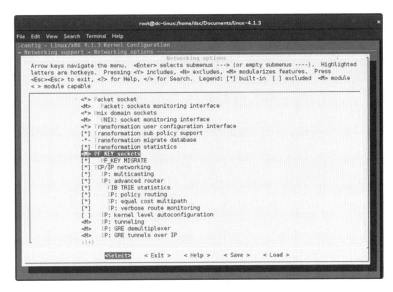

Above: Some of the range of network protocols can be seen on this kernel configuration application.

LET'S GET STARTED

We're therefore going to work on the premise that we want to connect to an Ethernet network using IP. Our test network is pretty much the same as most people have at home on their broadband connections: there's a router that connects to the broadband link itself, and this router usually has both a handful of Ethernet ports and the ability to talk wireless networking too.

Hot Tip

Even if you're not going to use them, check out the list of networking options and read up on some of them on the internet. It's fascinating stuff, honest!

In order to use an IP network, our Linux machine needs to be configured with three things:

- An IP address.
- The address of its default gateway.
- The address of one or more Domain Name Service (DNS) servers.

Home_EXT	
Details	Signal Strength **Good**
Security	Link speed **28 Mb/s**
Identity	Security **WPA, WPA2**
IPv4	IPv4 Address **192.168.1.186**
IPv6	IPv6 Address **fe80::aeb5:7dff:fe65:8565**
Reset	Hardware Address **AC:B5:7D:65:85:65**
	Default Route **192.168.1.1**
	DNS **192.168.1.1**

Above: In this case, the router is the DNS.

You may have heard of a thing called IPv6 (which unsurprisingly means Internet Protocol Version 6), and you'll certainly come across it from time to time when you're exploring your Linux machine's configuration. The version of the Internet Protocol we've been using for years is called IPv4, and for our purposes, we only need to know about IPv4, since IPv6 is only really relevant at the moment if you're an Internet Service Provider or a much bigger company than most of us work for. An IPv4 address looks like 192.168.1.100 – four numbers separated by dots (this form is often called 'dotted quad' notation). The main thing you need to remember is that no two computers on the same network segment can have the same IP address.

Subnets

IP networks are split into segments called subnets (actually, there are loads of other terms as well, but if you talk of subnets, everyone will know what you mean). These are connected by routers. Note that we mentioned a few sentences ago that the average home network has a router connecting to the service provider. So if you're wondering ... yes, that home network is merely a subnet of the service provider's network, and your bit of the world is separated from theirs by the router. Computers are able to talk directly to other computers that sit on the same subnet. So as we're typing this sentence we have our Linux-based laptop, the MacBook Pro we're writing this on and a rather aged iMac all connected to the same subnet. The Linux laptop is connected via the network to a shared directory on the MacBook and the two machines are talking directly to each other. We could power off the router and, although the internet would be inaccessible, these two machines wouldn't lose touch with each other.

WHAT A ROUTER DOES

When a machine wants to talk to something outside its own subnet, though, it can't make a direct connection. The thing it wants to connect to could be anywhere in the world, after all. That's the router's job – to know how to route traffic so it reaches its destination.

Above: If we needed to add routes, we could do so in the network control panel.

Hot Tip

Get to grips with your router, because it's key to how your network works, and understanding what it does will help you a lot.

There are two types of route that a router knows about. First, we have specific routes: the big routers that sit within the Internet Service Providers' networks have connections to other service providers' networks, and they have big tables of routing information which are basically just lists of IP address ranges that say: 'To route to address range X, send it out of this link to this neighbouring router whose address is Y.' Second is the entry at the end of every routing table that's basically a catch-all entry that says: 'If the address we want isn't in the list of specific routes, send it to Z.' This last entry is called the default route, and the device with address Z is called the default gateway. (Strictly speaking, it's not a gateway, as that means something else, but that's what everyone calls it, so we'll stick with it).

Below: A typical modern wireless router.

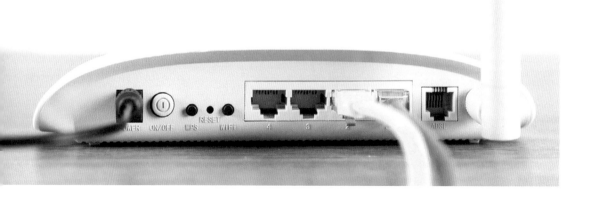

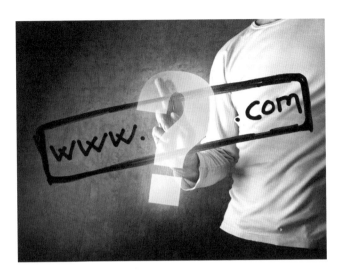

DOMAIN NAME SERVICE

Devices on the internet talk to each other by using numeric IP addresses. Humans are rubbish at remembering numbers though, so we like to have intuitive-sounding names. After all, would you prefer to type www.google.com into your browser or 212.9.14.121? The Domain Name Service, or DNS, is a mechanism for translating these names into addresses. It's run by thousands of DNS servers around the world, which act as a big distributed database. Our Linux machine's IP code knows how to contact a DNS server and how to interpret the results it receives, but it needs to know the IP address of at least one DNS server in order to know what to contact to ask the question.

HOW IT USUALLY WORKS

The Dynamic Host Configuration Protocol, or DHCP, is your best friend. When you connect a computer to your home network, you probably don't need to set any of the IP information we've mentioned – and that's because your router is a DHCP server. When a device starts up, it'll usually have DHCP addressing enabled by default. It broadcasts across the network to say: 'Can someone please give me an IP address?' and the router assigns one from its pool of free addresses. So most of the time, you don't have to do anything.

Hot Tip

Check out the 'DHCP Pool' of your broadband router – it'll show you the range of addresses it's been told to choose from and will usually show you which machines have been given which addresses.

Above: The wired network is currently off.

CONNECTING WITH ETHERNET

1. Let's connect our test machine, then. We've hooked it into the router with an Ethernet cable and fired it up. Now, if we go to the top right of the screen, we can see that the wired entry is saying that it's off, and that there's a little cross through the icon of a network connection (*see* left).

2. Click the arrow to the right and another menu appears (*see* right).

Above: The wired network is ready to connect.

3. We can click 'Connect', and since our router is a DHCP server it'll assign an address. Once Linux thinks the connection's working correctly we'll get a new network port icon in the top right of the window (*see* below).

4. Clicking again on the triangle icon in the top right, we can pull down the wired menu and select 'Wired Settings' to see what the server has assigned us (*see* opposite).

Below: A new network port icon has now appeared in the top right.

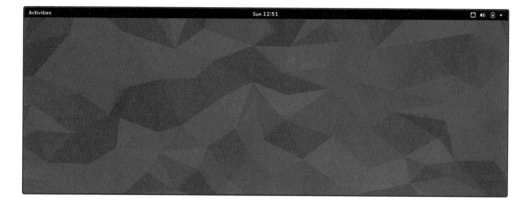

This is telling us, then, that we've been assigned:

- An IPv4 address of 192.168.1.173
- A default route of 192.168.1.1
- A DNS server of 192.168.1.1

5. Now, we happen to know that our router has the IP address 192.168.1.1 – not surprising given the default route. Like many small routers, the device is able to act as a DNS server, and so it's told our Linux machine to use it for DNS name-to-address look-ups.

Above: Wired Settings assigned by the server.

MANUAL CONFIGURATION

And if we don't have a DHCP server on our router? Simple. We need to set up the addresses manually, by going to 'Wired Settings' again, clicking 'Add Profile', selecting 'IPv4' in the left-hand pane, and adding our information by hand by selecting 'Manual' in the addresses pull-down and switching the automatic toggle on the DNS to off (see right).

But beware: as we've mentioned, you need to make sure that there's only one device on the network using any given IP address. In our test we tried setting our Fedora machine with an address that was the same as another device and it didn't complain at all. Duplicate addresses will make your systems work unpredictably, so be careful if you're using manual addresses.

Hot Tip
Your broadband router usually also acts as the DNS server, so it's perfectly normal to see the default route and the DNS server set to the same thing.

Above: Setting up the addresses manually.

SETTING WIRELESS

So, we've made our Linux machine talk to the world using cabled connections, but of course most people who are using Linux on desktop or laptop machines won't want to be tied down – literally – to their cabled networks. Wireless is, then, the order of the day.

EARLY WIRELESS

Linux's early history of wireless support was, frankly, appalling. This was primarily because there were various vendors of wireless network adaptors and they were too busy concentrating on just making it work to be able to spend time either producing Linux drivers or giving significant

help to the open source community. In fact, thinking back to those days, the whole wireless field was a bit wobbly in its infancy, because there were a few different strands to the development of the protocols, and it was somewhat unclear which way things would go. However, that's probably to be expected, as happens in many technological fields.

Once wireless came of age and became well established, Linux started to catch up in its ability to use it. And today, wireless is just as well supported as cabled Ethernet connectivity by the Linux producers.

WIRELESS TECHNOLOGIES

The technology standards for wireless networking come under the IEEE802.11 range of specifications. The initial developments were split largely into two streams: one using 2.4GHz radios and one using 5GHz radios. The main ones you'll come across are:

```
dsc@linuxpc-local:~

File  Edit  View  Search  Terminal  Help
[dsc@linuxpc-local ~]$ lspci
00:00.0 Host bridge: Intel Corporation Haswell-ULT DRAM Controller (rev 0b)
00:02.0 VGA compatible controller: Intel Corporation Haswell-ULT Integrated Graphics Controller (rev 0b)
00:03.0 Audio device: Intel Corporation Haswell-ULT HD Audio Controller (rev 0b)
00:14.0 USB controller: Intel Corporation 8 Series USB xHCI HC (rev 04)
00:16.0 Communication controller: Intel Corporation 8 Series HECI #0 (rev 04)
00:1b.0 Audio device: Intel Corporation 8 Series HD Audio Controller (rev 04)
00:1c.0 PCI bridge: Intel Corporation 8 Series PCI Express Root Port 3 (rev e4)
00:1c.3 PCI bridge: Intel Corporation 8 Series PCI Express Root Port 4 (rev e4)
00:1d.0 USB controller: Intel Corporation 8 Series USB EHCI #1 (rev 04)
00:1f.0 ISA bridge: Intel Corporation 8 Series LPC Controller (rev 04)
00:1f.2 SATA controller: Intel Corporation 8 Series SATA Controller 1 [AHCI mode] (rev 04)
00:1f.3 SMBus: Intel Corporation 8 Series SMBus Controller (rev 04)
01:00.0 Unassigned class [ff00]: Realtek Semiconductor Co., Ltd. Device 5287 (rev 01)
01:00.1 Ethernet controller: Realtek Semiconductor Co., Ltd. RTL8111/8168/8411 PCI Express Gigabit Ethernet Controller (rev 12)
02:00.0 Network controller: Qualcomm Atheros QCA9565 / AR9565 Wireless Network Adapter (rev 01)
[dsc@linuxpc-local ~]$
```

Above: We can use lspci to find out what wireless adapter we have. Once we know this, it is easy to search on the internet for its capabilities.

- 802.11b: The first mainstream 2.4GHz implementation, with a top speed of 11Mbit/s.

- 802.11a: The first mainstream 5GHz implementation, with a top speed of 54Mbit/s; although it came out around the same time as 802.11b it was more expensive, so most small installations went for the slower but significantly cheaper option.

- 802.11g: An evolution of the 2.4GHz approach, which brought the top speed up to match the 54Mbit/s of 802.11a.

- 802.11n: Applied to both radio speeds, and providing link speeds up to 72Mbit/s on a single channel (plus the ability to aggregate channels for higher speeds).

- 802.11ac: Another 5GHz implementation, ratified in 2014, aimed at bringing speeds up into several hundreds of megabits per second to keep wireless in line with the kind of speeds we see in cabled networks.

What This Means for Us

Simple: we find that the wireless LAN adaptors in laptops – particularly the cheaper ones – tend to support the 2.4GHz radios more than they do 5GHz ones. For example, our test laptop's spec sheet says that it supports 802.11b, 802.11g and 802.11n – no 5GHz radios for us, then.

As for Linux itself though, we're concerned with something more fundamental: whether or not the actual wireless adaptor is supported by our Linux distro (or, more accurately, the kernel at the core of it). Unless you have a really super-innovative laptop, this isn't usually a problem.

Wireless Speeds in Real Life

Before we get into the configuration side of wireless, a quick note of caution: wireless networks like air, and they don't like doors and walls. So if we connect our test laptop to the wireless service of the main router, which is about ten yards away and the other side of an internal wall, we see it connect at only 13Mbit/s (see right).

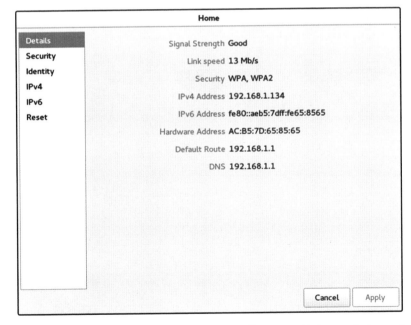

Above: The main router connects at only 13Mbit/s when there is a wall between it and the laptop wanting to connect.

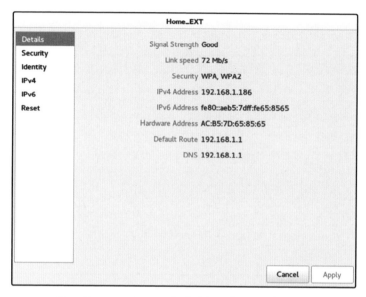

Home_EXT	
Details	Signal Strength **Good**
Security	Link speed **72 Mb/s**
Identity	Security **WPA, WPA2**
IPv4	IPv4 Address **192.168.1.186**
IPv6	IPv6 Address **fe80::aeb5:7dff:fe65:8565**
Reset	Hardware Address **AC:B5:7D:65:85:65**
	Default Route **192.168.1.1**
	DNS **192.168.1.1**

Cancel | Apply

Above: If you connect an extender, the link speed increases dramatically.

We do, however, have a wireless extender installed, which is about three yards from the desk with less brickwork in the way. Connect to this and we see 72Mbit/s (*see left*).

If you're having trouble with your wireless network connection, don't just think it's Linux playing up. Sit yourself down next to the router and try it, just to make sure the problem's not one of signal strength. And use an extender to deal with dark spots (we have TP-Link and NetGear ones – both very good).

Hot Tip
Take the time to check out your wireless signal strength and buy extenders – they're cheap and will make an enormous difference.

CONFIGURING THE WIRELESS CONNECTION

Setting up the wireless connection on Linux is very simple. In fact, you'll recall we did it back when we were going through the installation process, so we won't bore you with the same screenshots again. We will, however, talk about a couple of additional things that are useful to know.

HIDDEN NETWORKS

Most routers with wireless capabilities will advertise the networks they support. We saw this when we were getting ready to install, and we were able to pick from a list of available networks (*see* below).

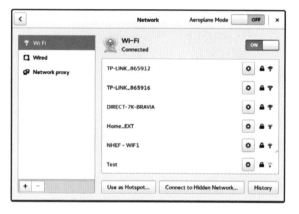

Above: You can pick from a list of networks that can be connected to.

Above: Once you've entered the name and details, the hidden WiFi connects just like it would to any other wireless network.

Some people prefer to keep their wireless networks hidden so you can't see them so easily. In a security sense, it's largely a waste of time (all you need is a free wireless sniffer tool and you'll spot them even though they're hidden), but you do come across the concept from time to time. To connect to a network of this sort, you simply need to go into the bit of the control panel that lets you configure things manually.

On Fedora 22, you go into the WiFi settings section and click 'Connect to Hidden Network...' – a pop-up appears that lets you enter the network name, select the type of security it's using and provide the security key (*see* left).

WIRELESS SECURITY

We mentioned in the last section that when configuring a hidden network, you select the type of security it's using. When you're connecting to a network that's being advertised to you, there's no need to do this, and that's because the Linux machine can deduce the security mechanism that's in place and hence it doesn't ask you.

The type of security in use is dictated not by the Linux machine but by the device hosting the network – your router, or wireless extender, or wireless access point. Whatever that's configured to use, you'll be able to use on your Linux PC.

There's a simple rule with wireless security: never, ever use WEP (Wired Equivalent Privacy). WEP is a very, very old standard and although its name suggests that it makes the wireless connection as secure as a wired one (that is, one that connects via an Ethernet cable) this simply isn't the case. Technology, which includes security technology, has marched on and WEP simply isn't considered secure any more, because it's really easy to break using modern computers.

Hot Tip

If you choose WEP as your wireless security, it's the equivalent of replacing your front door with a sheet of soggy paper. Just don't do it.

The Keys to Security

Wireless security has two components: authentication and encryption. The authentication component is there to check that you are authorized to use the network. In corporate environments, this can be done using advanced techniques that exchange secure keys and authenticate your computer against the company's core network systems. For normal users and small businesses though, this generally means using a passcode of some sort (preferably a complex one that's not easy to guess).

The encryption component is designed to make sure nobody can see what data is flowing over your wireless network. Given that you're using a radio to broadcast everything for quite some distance around you, it's sensible to encrypt the data you're throwing around.

You'll generally have three options for authentication: WEP, WPA (WiFi Protected Access) and WPA2. WPA2 is the newest and, unsurprisingly, the most secure.

Similarly, there are two common options for encrypting the data: TKIP (Temporal Key Integrity Protocol) and AES (Advanced Encryption Standard). AES is considered the more secure.

Hot Tip

WPA2 with AES encryption is the way to go if your router supports it.

Before you start connecting your Linux workstation to the network, then, check out the configuration of the network and switch it to WPA2 and AES if your kit supports it. Don't be surprised if this isn't the case: the router our Internet Service Provider gave us doesn't do AES, for example. If that's the case, go with an alternative (but don't touch WEP).

Below: WPA2 and AES are the more secure options for WiFi.

TELNET AND PORT CONFIGURATION

So far, then, we've looked at how you get connected to the network. Once you're hooked up, you can do all the obvious things like browsing the internet and connecting to shared folders on the other computers in your house or office. But what if you want to use your Linux machine as a server of some sort?

Even if you're not going to run a live website on your server (there are plenty of companies out there who will host your site for you at little charge), it's common to want to be able to develop stuff on a machine of your own so you can test it fully on your internal machine before sending

it to the live server in a hosting centre somewhere. That's exactly what we do with the web services we work with when we're not writing books on Linux. So let's look at how this works.

TCP

TCP is part of the IP protocol family. It stands for Transmission Control Protocol, and it's used by the vast majority of programs that provide some kind of networked service. It has a sister called UDP, or the User Datagram Protocol, which is a bit more niche, but still relevant as it's used by stuff like voice calls and streamed video – and the DNS service we discussed earlier, in fact (see page 189). We'll focus mainly on TCP though.

Below: The 'services' file lists commonly known TCP ports.

```
# /etc/services:
# $Id: services,v 1.55 2013/04/14 ovasik Exp $
#
# Network services, Internet style
# IANA services version: last updated 2013-04-10
#
# Note that it is presently the policy of IANA to assign a single well-known
# port number for both TCP and UDP; hence, most entries here have two entries
# even if the protocol doesn't support UDP operations.
# Updated from RFC 1700, ``Assigned Numbers'' (October 1994).  Not all ports
# are included, only the more common ones.
#
# The latest IANA port assignments can be gotten from
#        http://www.iana.org/assignments/port-numbers
# The Well Known Ports are those from 0 through 1023.
# The Registered Ports are those from 1024 through 49151
# The Dynamic and/or Private Ports are those from 49152 through 65535
#
# Each line describes one service, and is of the form:
#
# service-name  port/protocol  [aliases ...]   [# comment]

tcpmux          1/tcp                           # TCP port service multiplexer
tcpmux          1/udp                           # TCP port service multiplexer
rje             5/tcp                           # Remote Job Entry
rje             5/udp                           # Remote Job Entry
echo            7/tcp
echo            7/udp
discard         9/tcp           sink null
discard         9/udp           sink null
systat          11/tcp          users
systat          11/udp          users
```

A TCP connection from a client machine to a server machine is not unlike a phone call. The client initiates a call (a connection to us) and when the server sees the request come in, it answers it. The client and server can then exchange information as they see fit, and then when they're done, either of the parties can close the connection.

Hot Tip

Read up about TCP and IP – they're the absolute fundamentals of networking, these days, and even an hour or two's reading up on them will help greatly.

You probably want the server to be able to accept more than one call at once – akin to it having several phones that people can call into. Furthermore, you probably want some way for it to know what kind of call is coming in so that you can have, say, the web server answering only web requests and the email server answering email connections. TCP uses the concept of a port for this.

HOW TCP PORTS WORK

When the client device tries to set up a connection, there are two key components to the request. First, and pretty obvious, is the IP address of the system it's trying to connect to. Second is the port number it wants to connect to, which is a number between 0 and 65,535.

When a program such as a web server starts up, it 'listens' for incoming connections on the network link. The trick is though, that the software will only listen on a specific port or ports. Imagine you have a phone system with 65,536 extensions; you have the same number of telephones and you've labelled each of them with a number from 0 to 65,535. Any of them could ring at any time, but you've told the web server only to answer extension 80, and the mail server only to answer extension 25. That's precisely what happens with Linux server software.

Well-known Ports

Ports 0 to 1023 are called well-known ports, and have been assigned to core, general functions: web and email servers, remote connectivity etc. Some of the common ports are:

- 22: SSH, the secure shell mechanism that lets you connect into the Linux machine and use a command line to run commands and programs.

- 25: SMTP, the Simple Mail Transfer Protocol (internet email, basically).

- 53: DNS, the Domain Name Service.

- 80: HTTP, the HyperText Transfer Protocol (web servers).

- 109 and 110: POP, for pulling email down from a server.

- 443: HTTPS, the high-secure version of HTTP.

Hot Tip

Don't be frightened by all these numbers – in no time at all, you'll find you know that port 80 is for the web server, and so on.

```
                                    root@linuxpc-local:~

 File  Edit  View  Search  Terminal  Help
[root@linuxpc-local ~]# netstat -nlt
Active Internet connections (only servers)
Proto Recv-Q Send-Q Local Address          Foreign Address        State
tcp        0      0 0.0.0.0:445            0.0.0.0:*              LISTEN
tcp        0      0 0.0.0.0:139            0.0.0.0:*              LISTEN
tcp        0      0 0.0.0.0:22             0.0.0.0:*              LISTEN
tcp        0      0 127.0.0.1:631          0.0.0.0:*              LISTEN
tcp6       0      0 :::443                 :::*                  LISTEN
tcp6       0      0 :::445                 :::*                  LISTEN
tcp6       0      0 :::139                 :::*                  LISTEN
tcp6       0      0 :::80                  :::*                  LISTEN
tcp6       0      0 :::22                  :::*                  LISTEN
tcp6       0      0 ::1:631                :::*                  LISTEN
[root@linuxpc-local ~]# ▌
```

Above: The netstat command shows what ports we're listening on.

Root Super User

The above well-known ports are special in that if you're running a Unix or Linux machine you have to be the root super user to run a program that listens on one of them. This is useful if you have a multi-purpose server, because a normal user can't randomly run up their own mail or web server on a well-known port and break something.

Other Ports

Just a quick note before we carry on: there's nothing to stop you running a server program on a port other than its standard well-known port. These are, however, the default ports that client software will use. So for example, if we enter this URL in our web browser:

www.mysupplier.com

... the browser will use the DNS to look up the IP address of the machine called www.mysupplier.com and will attempt to connect to it on port 80, because it knows that's the usual port for a web server. If the web server's running on a different port, you have to access it in a different way. It's common, for example, to have a test version on the same server on a different port such as 8080, in which case, the user would have to specify the port in the URL:

www.mysupplier.com:8080

Registered Ports

Ports 1,024 to 49,151 are called registered ports. These have been registered with a central agency as being officially assigned to specific applications produced by specific vendors. So for example, IBM's Notes email server uses port 1,352 and Windows Live Messenger used port 1,503 before it was discontinued by Microsoft. You don't have to be a super user to use these.

The Rest

Ports above 49,151 are available for anyone to use as they see fit.

Hot Tip

Nobody really cares about the demarcation at 49,151 – all we really care about is whether it's privileged (below 1,024) or non-privileged (1,024 and above).

GET AN APPLICATION

Your Linux machine can't magically become, say, a web server without running a web server program, of course. Point a browser at a newly installed Linux machine and it'll fail to connect.

You'll need to do two things to make it happen: get a web server program, and ensure any onboard firewall software is configured to let connections in.

Below: The web server connection has been refused.

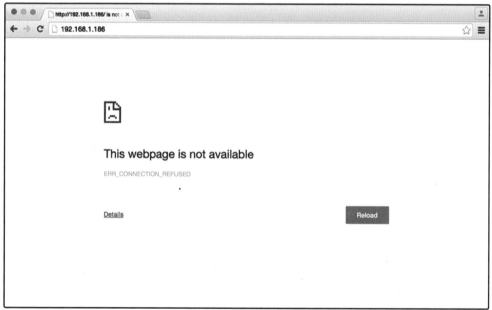

This webpage is not available

ERR_CONNECTION_REFUSED

Details

Reload

The most popular web server program is Apache, and it's a dead-easy to obtain it for our Fedora server with dnf install HTTPD. Note, by the way, that HTTPD stands for HyperText Transfer Protocol Daemon; a daemon in Unix/Linux terms is basically a program that sits constantly running in the background answering requests.

Once we've obtained it, we need to start it up. We'll use systemctl for that.

```
[root@dc-linux ~]# systemctl start httpd
```

Now if we try to connect to the web server again from our client machine, we'll have more luck ... or will we?

Below: An error message indicates we are still unable to connect.

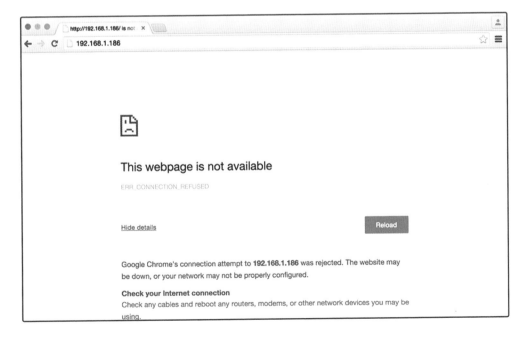

Hang about. What's going on? We've started the web server program, and we can use the ps command to check that it's running:

```
[root@dc-linux ~]# ps ax | grep httpd
6050 ?        Ss     0:00 /usr/sbin/httpd -DFOREGROUND
6109 ?        S      0:00 /usr/sbin/httpd -DFOREGROUND
6111 ?        S      0:00 /usr/sbin/httpd -DFOREGROUND
6112 ?        S      0:00 /usr/sbin/httpd -DFOREGROUND
6113 ?        S      0:00 /usr/sbin/httpd -DFOREGROUND
6114 ?        S      0:00 /usr/sbin/httpd -DFOREGROUND
```

IPTABLES

We've already mentioned that Linux is pretty inherently secure, and one of the things that contributes to this is the inclusion of the IPTables firewall software as part of the default installation. A firewall is a piece of software that acts as a barrier to incoming and outgoing connections and ensures that, regardless of what programs are running on the system, only the connections that the system administrator permits are allowed to happen. The out-of-the-box approach, quite sensibly, is for the system to permit a minimal set of connectivity. So let's run a quick IPTables command:

```
iptables -I INPUT 1 -p tcp -m state —state NEW -m tcp —dport 80 -j ACCEPT
```

This command is basically telling IPTables to add an 'input' rule (that is, for new inbound connections destined for this machine) using the TCP protocol, to destination port 80 (the web server port), and that it should accept those connections. Try again with our browser (see right).

That's more like it – the machine has answered our request and has sent us a test page to prove it's up. So let's tell the machine to save our new setting. IPTables won't save it unless we tell it to, so restarting the machine now would cause it to refuse connections after the restart.

(Actually, the Fedora documentation says the current ruleset is saved when IPTables shuts down but it's a fib, so we'll save the rules by hand):

```
[root@dc-linux ~]# iptables-save >
/etc/sysconfig/iptables
```

IPTables isn't for the faint-hearted. The commands are cryptic and some of what it does can be puzzling unless you're really comfortable with how IP networking works. Happily for the kind of stuff you're likely to be doing as a Linux beginner, there's enough information out there in Googleland to help you do most of what you need, and there's nothing to stop you checking out the man page and using a bit of trial and error.

Below: The web server is now working correctly.

Hot Tip

IPTables is your friend, but it's the easiest thing in the world to forget to save the settings! Make sure your changes work okay then be sure to save, or it won't work after a restart.

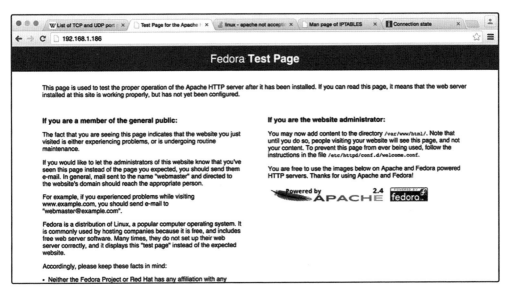

LINUX AS A SERVER

CONFIGURING A PERSONAL NAS (NETWORK ATTACHED STORAGE) SERVER

Linux is hugely popular as a server – that is, a machine that hosts some kind of service such as file storage, printer co-ordination, a database, an email transport system or a web server.

For internet-facing servers (e.g. corporate web servers) the numbers are vast: in the July 2015 Netcraft Web Server Survey (http://news.netcraft.com/archives/2015/07/22/july-2015-web-server-survey.html), just over 325 million servers were detected worldwide running the Apache web server software, and it's a safe bet that the vast majority of these are Linux-based. Serious numbers, then.

SHARE FILES

Linux servers don't have to be public-facing. It's common, for instance, to want to have some kind of system at home that you can use to store your files so you can either keep a back-up copy or, more commonly, have them shared among the family. And people who host their own websites out on the internet will generally have some kind of home

machine to do their development on, so they can
get everything just right before uploading the code
to the internet. We'll look at a couple of the
common things people do, then.

NETWORK FILE SYSTEM

First, we'll look at how to run up a fileserver using a
Linux machine. Now, we could use a thing called NFS
(Network File System), because this is the native file-sharing protocol for Unix-style systems
such as Linux. The thing is that not many people have machines that support NFS – we're all
Windows or Mac users. Since the majority of machines connecting to our server will be
Windows PCs, we'll go with the Windows standard, which is variously called SMB (Server
Message Block) or CIFS (Common Internet File System) – and we're not alienating Mac or Linux
clients by doing this, because they can both access SMB file shares.

DOING THE SAMBA

On Linux, SMB is implemented using the Samba package, which originated in 1992 and was a massive hit right from the start. This is a standard part of the Fedora installation on our test machine, and although we've shown some of our examples using command line instructions, we'll show some of this one with the graphical configuration interface. Well, it's friendlier than typing commands, so why not?

BEFORE WE START

In order to run the configuration process, we have to be able to run administrator-level functions. There are two ways to do this:

- Log in as the 'root' user on the Linux machine before you start the configuration process.

- Log in as a user that you've created as an 'Administrator'.

For this example, we've logged in as 'root'.

OUR SHARING SETUP

The setup we'll go with is fairly basic: we'll create the user 'max', and he'll have his own personal directory that's private to him. Once you've got your basic Samba setup working, this is 95 per cent of the battle won – if you then want to go on and start playing with shared directories and the like, you won't find it overly difficult.

CREATE THE USER

A much less faffy way to create a user is simply to use the user add command to do all of the above in a couple of commands. First, the user creation:

```
[root@fileserver-local ~]# useradd -c 'Max Cooter' max
```

Now we'll set the password:

```
[root@fileserver-local ~]# passwd max
Changing password for user max.
New password:
Retype new password:
passwd: all authentication tokens updated successfully.
```

SETTING UP SAMBA

If you don't have Samba installed, get out your package manager and install it (dnf install Samba for us). We do this by editing the file 'smb.conf' in the '/etc' directory, which we can do with the Files feature in the Activities menu – just scroll to the right file and double-click it.

The config file looks scary – but don't panic! You only have to edit a very small number of bits in order to get going. We're going to configure our server as a stand-alone machine (because it is – it's not part of a corporate directory service). We'll put it in workgroup 'LINUXWG' and we'll call the machine 'LINUXSVR'. So in the 'smb.conf' directory, we just look for the lines that match the left-hand side (the bit before the '=' sign) of each of these and update the right-hand side. Don't randomly throw them in, or it's unlikely to work – the config file is in sections and you're likely to put things in the wrong place. Note also that you'll find some lines that look like these but which start with a ';' or a '#'. These are comments, so they won't work unless you remove the leading ';' or '#'.

Hot Tip

Check your address range and make sure the Samba config has been told to allow connections from it, otherwise you'll be scratching your head when the machine can connect to itself but nothing else can get in.

```
workgroup = LINUXWG
netbios name = LINUXSVR
hosts allow = 127. 192.
security = user
passdb backend = tbdsam
```

Note the third line here – it's a list of IP address ranges that the Samba server allows in. We've told it to allow any device whose IP address starts with '127.' (this is a special address called the 'loopback', and you always include this) or '192.'. If your local computers' IPs start with something else ('10.' isn't unusual, for instance), then list it in here or your systems won't connect.

SPECIAL USERS

Before we can carry on, there's a catch: Samba uses its own password file if you're running on a stand-alone machine as we are, and so you'll need to tell it about our new user. We do this with the 'smbpasswd' command:

```
[root@fileserver-local samba]# smbpasswd -a max
New SMB password:
Retype new SMB password:
Added user max.
```

In more complex setups you can have a directory service to which Samba and all your other systems authenticate, but that's for another day (and another book).

GETTING US THROUGH THE FIREWALL

When we've done other network tasks, we've had to play with the IPTables firewall settings in order to get our Linux server to allow incoming connections. Samba's no exception – as it stands our Samba software will sit waiting for connections, but the IPTables function will stop inbound connections getting as far as the Samba program. So let's add some rules and then save them to the start-up settings:

```
[root@fileserver]# iptables -I INPUT 1 -m state —state NEW -p
tcp —dport 137 -j ACCEPT
[root@fileserver]# iptables -I INPUT 1 -m state —state NEW -p
tcp —dport 138 -j ACCEPT
[root@fileserver]# iptables -I INPUT 1 -m state —state NEW -p
tcp —dport 139 -j ACCEPT
[root@fileserver]# iptables -I INPUT 1 -m state —state NEW -p
tcp —dport 445 -j ACCEPT
[root@fileserver]# iptables-save > /etc/sysconfig/iptables
```

Now we can start Samba:

```
[root@fileserver]# systemctl start smb ; systemctl start nmb
```

Hot Tip

Remember that Samba doesn't magically read from Linux's own user database – it'll be a head-scratching session if you forget!

SELINUX

There's one more thing though, and it may or may not be installed on your Linux machine. Another of the standard security features with many Linux distributions, including the one on our Fedora 22 machine, is SELinux – short for 'Security Enhanced Linux'. This is a security module that's part of the kernel and which watches for nefarious activity. One of the things it generally blocks by default is Samba's use of home directories, so let's tell it to allow them:

```
[root@fileserver]# setsebool -P samba_enable_home_dirs on
```

TRYING IT OUT

Okay, now we think we have our Samba server running, we can check it with a very cool widget called 'smbclient'. This is part of the Samba installation, and it lets us probe our machine to see if it can see our Samba services being advertised. We run it in the terminal window on the Linux machine using the '-L' flag to tell it to connect to 'localhost' (itself) and we'll use the '-U' flag to tell it we want to connect as user 'max'. It'll ask for Max's password, then tell us what it can see:

```
[root@fileserver-local samba]# smbclient -L localhost -U max
Enter max's password:
Domain=[LINUXWG] OS=[Windows 6.1] Server=[Samba 4.2.2]

        Sharename       Type        Comment
        ---------       ----        -------
        IPC$            IPC         IPC Service (Samba Server Version 4.2.2)
        max             Disk        Home Directories
Domain=[LINUXWG] OS=[Windows 6.1] Server=[Samba 4.2.2]
        Server                      Comment
        --------                    --------
        LINUXSVR                    Samba Server Version 4.2.2

        Workgroup                   Master
        --------                    --------
        LINUXWG                     LINUXSVR
```

The key things here are that we can see that we have server 'LINUXSVR' and workgroup 'LINUXWG'. In the Sharename section at the top, we can see that 'max' is a share that's available to us. So then, let's have a go at connecting to the server from our Mac. Let's fire up the 'Connect to Server' option and enter the name of our fileshare – smb://linuxsvr/ (*see* right).

If the server is available, it'll ask us to log in – and if it isn't, we'll get an error. So it's a promising sign if we see the login box – we'll enter our details and hit 'Connect' (*see* middle right).

Give it a moment to connect and we can use our shared folder just like any other (*see* bottom right).

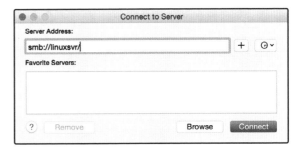

Above: Once you've entered the name of the fileshare, you should be able to connect to the server.

Above: Enter your details in the login box.

Above: Our shared folder.

Hot Tip

'smbclient' is your friend – it's a brilliant way to verify that your Samba configuration is working correctly and advertising the fileshares you want to advertise.

USING THE APACHE WEB SERVER

We mentioned earlier that Apache is a hugely popular web server; what we didn't mention is that it's the most popular in the world by a long way.

So the 325 million or so Apache installations in the survey we cited represents about 38 per cent of the servers the survey has found; Microsoft's server offering has a mere 27 per cent or so, and thus is some way behind. We've done the basics of how to get an Apache server working (see pages 209–211), so in this section we'll go into a bit more depth and show you how to do some more interesting stuff with your Apache server.

IT'S CALLED 'HTTPD'

There was a time when Apache referred only to the web server software of that name. Over the years though, the Apache project has expanded vastly and now has a shedload of different applications under its umbrella. The HTTPD (HyperText Transfer Protocol Daemon), as it's called, is the web server package – and every reference you come across on your Linux machine talks about the HTTPD in some way.

So for instance, you start, stop and restart the server by referencing the 'httpd' service:

```
[root@fileserver]# systemctl start httpd
[root@fileserver]# systemctl enable httpd
[root@fileserver]# systemctl stop httpd
```

CONFIGURING THE SERVER

The configuration file is the main thing you'll fiddle with, and it's called 'httpd.conf'. On our Fedora machine, it's located in directory '/etc/httpd/conf/', and as it's a text file, we can simply navigate using the Files tool and double-click it to fire it up in a text editor.

Don't Be Afraid of the Config File

You'll find that Linux configuration files look quite scary – as we saw with the Samba config file earlier. But as we've said, it's really nothing to worry about because the settings that it comes with 'out of the box' are generally enough either to get up and running or at least come close. As we saw in the previous chapter, the Apache web server gives you a 'Hey, I'm working' test page as soon as you've fired it up and told the firewall to let the connections through – no configuration

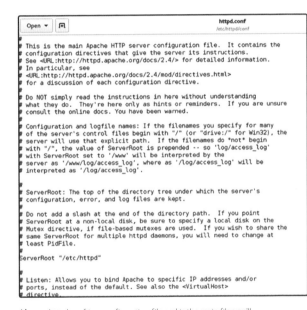

Above: httpd.conf is a configuration file and is the main file you'll use to set up the server.

Hot Tip

Knowing your way around httpd.conf is a handy thing – explore the one that ships with your machine and read the comments to understand what it's doing.

required. This is a great place to start, because if you begin with something that works, you can change the config one item at a time and if it breaks, you simply undo the last thing you did and try again.

WHERE THE PAGES LIVE

If you check the config file, you'll see a setting for 'DocumentRoot':

```
DocumentRoot "/var/www/html"
```

So in this case, we see that '/var/www/html' is where our documents live. Navigate there with the Files tool and we see the contents, which in a plain installation is nothing!

The server will give you the 'Hey, I'm working' page if you haven't put a file in there for it to read. Now, let's check out the 'Directory Index' line in the config file:

Above: Navigate to '/var/www/html' to see the 'DocumentRoot'.

```
DirectoryIndex index.html
```

The way web servers work is that if the URL (web address) you enter in the browser ends in a '/', the server will look for some kind of default file. The DirectoryIndex setting here is telling us that it'll try to look for a file called 'index.html'. So let's create a simple one:

```
<HTML>
 <HEAD><TITLE>Test
page</TITLE></HEAD>
 <BODY>
 <h1>Test title</h1>
  This is a test.
 </BODY>
</HTML>
```

Now we have our index file in the directory (*see* above right).

Above: You can now see the index file in the 'DocumentRoot'.

Let's fire up the browser and point it at our machine. Its IP address is 192.168.1.186, so we use URL 'http://192.168.1.186' and watch it find 'index.html' (*see* right).

Not the prettiest test page, we'll grant you, but believe us, it's very cool the first time you achieve it.

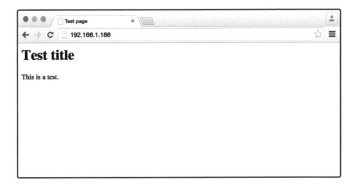

Above: The computer finds the 'index.html' file we made earlier.

OVER TO YOU

Now you've seen the basics of what you need to get going, the sky is the limit. Start making your pages, and take it a step at a time – you'll surprise yourself at how quickly you progress.

Hot Tip

Play with documents and links – you're not going to break anything by doing so. When you need to do more than just plan HTML documents, check out the PHP programming language.

GENERATING SELF-SIGNED CERTIFICATES AND SSL-PROTECTED WEBSITES

We've given you a start on getting your web server up and running, but there's one more key component that's essential to commercial websites – secure web connectivity. By this, we mean HTTPS – the secure version of HTTP.

For HTTPS to work, we need what's called a digital certificate. This is an electronic 'key' (which is basically a text file full of heavily encrypted information) which does two things: it allows the browser to authenticate the server (that is, confirm that the server is who it says it is); and it provides information that allows the browser and the server to encrypt data as it's sent to and fro, in order that an intruder can't simply tap into it and read the data streams.

SSL CERTIFICATES

You'll find, incidentally, that these certificates are often referred to as 'SSL certificates'. SSL is the Secure Sockets Layer, one of the standard security mechanisms used in networking for donkey's years now. In reality, SSL has been superseded by TLS (Transport Layer Security). There are differences, but you can work on the premise that whether someone talks about SSL certificates, digital certificates or (less often) TLS certificates, they're basically talking about the same thing.

Let's have a quick bit of background, then on to how we get our Apache server working with a digital certificate. And note that as with the stuff we've already done on Samba and other configuration settings, it looks scary but it's not.

Self-signed Certificates

Commercial websites have commercial security certificates. The benefit of these is that they're provided by trusted certification authorities (CAs) and so the user of the website knows that the website belongs to whom it says it does. For our purposes, we're going to stick with what's called a 'self-signed' certificate: this is a certificate that we generate ourselves and which, although it lets our web server work in true HTTPS fashion, will cause the browser to show some warnings due to it not being from a true CA. This isn't a problem though – it's how most people run their development web servers, not least because commercial certificates cost money (and lots of it).

Hot Tip
Certificates are complicated, but thankfully you don't actually need to know all that much about how they work, only what you need to do to create and install them.

CREATING THE ENCRYPTION STUFF

In order to run a secure web server, we need a digital certificate. As we've said, we're not going to get one from a CA but will generate our own. We'll do this by making the system generate a secure key, then generating a certificate request and then creating our own certificate from it. If you were using a CA you'd do the first two steps yourself, but then throw the certificate request at the CA for them to generate the certificate.

Before we start, we'll ensure that we have the necessary prerequisites. We already have Apache HTTPD but we need to ensure that the 'openssl', 'mod_ssl' and 'crypto-utils' packages are installed: as we've covered it already, we won't go into the detail of how to use 'dnf' for this.

Generating the Key

First, then, let's generate the key. In our example we'll use DES3 encryption and we'll tell it to generate a 2,048-bit key. This is pretty standard these days: the more bits you use the more secure it is, but the harder it is to process and hence the more your web server will slow down.

We use the `openssl` command to generate the key; it prompts for a password, which is used to secure the key itself – make sure you use a complex one and keep a safe note of it.

```
[root@local]## openssl genrsa -des3 -out linux.key 2048
Generating RSA private key, 2048 bit long modulus
................+++
.........................+++
e is 65537 (0x10001)
Enter pass phrase for linux.key:
Verifying - Enter pass phrase for linux.key:
```

Create the Certificate Request

Now we'll create the certificate request using the openssl command. It asks for some information about our organization; ours is invented, but if you're doing this with a CA-provided certificate, you'll need to be careful to enter correct, valid information. Why? Because the CA will demand that you prove who you are – so if you're a company and your registration document doesn't match what you've put in the certificate request, they'll tell you where to go.

```
[root@local]# openssl req -new -key linux.key -out linux.csr
Enter pass phrase for linux.key:
You are about to be asked to enter information that will be incorporated
into your certificate request.
What you are about to enter is what is called a Distinguished Name or a DN.
There are quite a few fields but you can leave some blank
For some fields there will be a default value,
If you enter '.', the field will be left blank.
-----
Country Name (2 letter code) [XX]:GB
State or Province Name (full name) []:Jersey
Locality Name (eg, city) [Default City]:St Helier
Organization Name (eg, company) [Default Company Ltd]:Linux Made Easy
Organizational Unit Name (eg, section) []:
Common Name (eg, your name or your server's hostname)
[]:www.mylinux.local
Email Address []:dsc@linuxmadeeasy.com

Please enter the following 'extra' attributes to be sent with your
certificate request
A challenge password []:
An optional company name []:
```

CREATING THE CERTIFICATE

Now we can create our certificate. Before we do, we have to do a special step and take off the password from the key file so the certificate generator can work with it:

```
[root@local]# mv linux.key linux.key.org
[root@local]# openssl rsa -in linux.key.org -out linux.key
Enter pass phrase for linux.key.org:
writing RSA key
```

And finally, we'll generate the certificate itself:

```
[root@local]# openssl x509 -req -days 90 -in linux.csr -
signkey linux.key -out linux.crt
Signature ok
subject=/C=GB/ST=Jersey/L=St Helier/O=Linux Made
Easy/CN=www.mylinux.local/emailAddress=dsc@linuxmadeeasy.com
Getting Private key
[root@fileserver-local html]#
```

Once we've done all this, we have four files. The basic encryption key is 'linux.key'. This was used to produce 'linux.csr', which is the certificate request. We then tweaked the key and kept 'linux.key.org', which was the original, just in case something went wrong (we don't need this any more). Finally, we have 'linux.crt', which is the certificate itself.

Hot Tip

If you do want to host a secure site, you'll need to get a certificate assigned by a CA, as you don't want people reading your page to get browser pop-ups telling them that the certificate isn't authorized.

CONFIGURING HTTPD

Now we've got all the bits we need, we can add it to the HTTPD configuration. To do this, we need to put the files somewhere sensible and then point the config file at them. We'll create a subdirectory 'ssl' in the HTTPD config directory and copy the key file and the certificate into it:

```
[root@local]# mkdir /etc/httpd/conf/ssl/
[root@local]# cp linux.crt /etc/httpd/conf/ssl/linux.crt
[root@local]# cp linux.key /etc/httpd/conf/ssl/linux.key
```

Now we need to edit 'httpd.conf' and tell it that (a) we want it to talk using the secure HTTP protocol, and (b) where to find its keys. We do this by adding a 'virtual host' entry (in our example, we dropped it in just after the "Listen 80" line of the config file):

```
# SSL config
<VirtualHost _default_:443>
    DocumentRoot /var/www/html
    ServerName www.mylinux.local
    SSLEngine on
    SSLCertificateFile /etc/httpd/conf/ssl/linux.crt
    SSLCertificateKeyFile /etc/httpd/conf/ssl/linux.key
</VirtualHost>
```

What this is basically telling HTTPD is:

- The website documents live in /var/www/html

- The server name is www.mylinux.local

- We want to turn on the SSL Engine (the module that provides secure functionality).

- The certificate file and key file are in the given locations with the specified names.

Because we've edited the configuration file, we need to restart HTTPD for it to see the changes:

```
root@local]# systemctl restart httpd
```

DON'T FORGET IPTABLES

Remember we had to tell IPTables to let connections come into our basic web server? Well, guess what … port 443 is the HTTPS port, so we need to add that to IPTables' permissions and save it for future reference.

```
[root@local]# iptables
-I INPUT 1 -p tcp -m state
—state NEW -m tcp —dport
443 -j ACCEPT
[root@local]# iptables-save
> /etc/sysconfig /iptables
```

And that's it. We can now access our server with an HTTPS connection in the browser. We expect it to complain that the certificate isn't one from a CA, of course (see right).

We can check the certificate information by clicking on the appropriate link in the browser – in our example, it does indeed show the details we entered a few pages back when we created the certificate. Click through the warning and we're in.

Above: The browser will come up with a security warning.

Above: Check that the certificate is correct.

Above: Our page is now SSL protected.

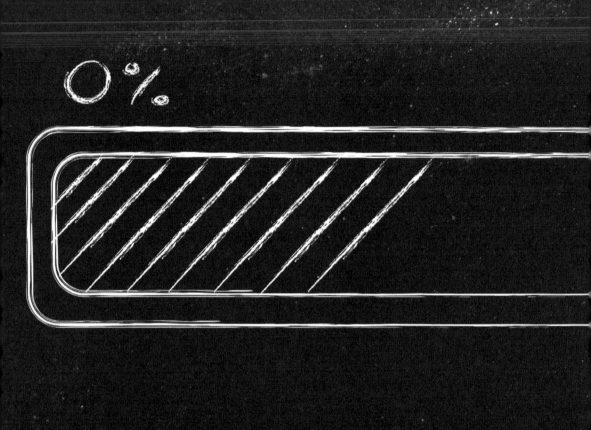

0%

LOADi

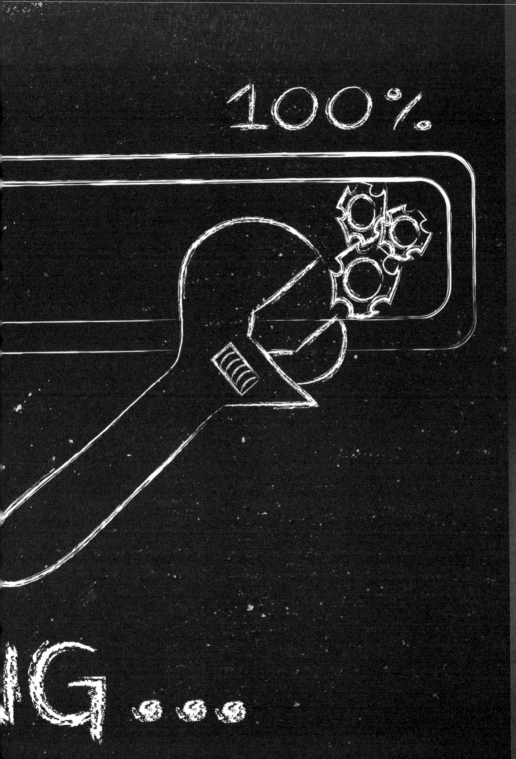

TROUBLESHOOTING AND GLOSSARY

WHAT TO DO WHEN THINGS GO WRONG

There will, of course, be a point at which something goes wrong. Linux is generally a very stable platform, but there's always the potential for problems – hardware giving up the ghost, perhaps, but more likely something user-inflicted (we'll come back to that concept later). It's not unusual to do something daft and break the configuration of the system, causing it to stop working, so what do we do when things go wrong?

IF YOU CAN'T GET IN REMOTELY

The most common problem with Linux is when the machine is up and running but you can't get in from a remote machine via SSH or some other remote tool. There could be a number of reasons for this: a dodgy network cable; the machine losing its IP settings; the system not enabling its LAN card correctly; an issue with the wireless network configuration (such as the authentication mechanism changing the machine's settings, hence no longer matching); the IPTables configuration having locked you out; or one of any number of other things.

The answer is to try to log in from the console of the machine itself. If you can't get in as a normal user, then click the 'Not listed' link on the login screen and try getting in as the root user.

IF IT STARTS BOOTING BUT DOESN'T FINISH

More common is where it starts booting but only gets partway in before giving some kind of error message. These are generally exemplified by the words 'kernel panic' somewhere in the plethora of error messages, or perhaps a message telling you that one or other of the disk volumes couldn't be mounted. The latter is common if the machine has crashed or you've

Hot Tip

It is possible for your user login to be corrupted. This could be a corruption in the user's configuration files or the shadow entry. The best way to figure this out is to log in as a different user.

powered it down rather than shutting it down gracefully. Although the file system formats on today's Linux are much more robust and resilient to forced shutdowns than they were, you still sometimes get to the stage where it says: 'I'm not carrying on until I've had this disk cleaned up.'

If this happens, you can try to boot the machine in single-user mode and run a file system check on the disk it says is corrupted. You do this by:

○ Pressing 'e' on the start-up screen so you can edit the boot command before it executes.

○ Scrolling down to the line that tells the system how to start up (it'll have 'vmlinuz' mentioned in it), then adding a space followed by the word 'single' at the end.

○ Pressing CTRL-X to continue booting.

Below: fsck lets us check and fix filesystems if we've got problems.

```
root@localhost:~                                               ✕

File  Edit  View  Search  Terminal  Help
[root@localhost ~]# fsck /dev/sda2
fsck from util-linux 2.26.2
fsck.fat 3.0.27 (2014-11-12)
0x41: Dirty bit is set. Fs was not properly unmounted and some data may be corru
pt.
1) Remove dirty bit
2) No action
? 2
There are differences between boot sector and its backup.
This is mostly harmless. Differences: (offset:original/backup)
  65:01/00
1) Copy original to backup
2) Copy backup to original
3) No action
? 2
```

The system will start up in a text-only mode, prompt you for the root password, then give you a command prompt. You can then run basic commands, the common one being `fsck`, the file system check tool, on the volume it previously told you was broken.

IF THIS DOESN'T HELP

If you can't get the system to boot into single-user mode, the easiest thing to do is boot from a USB stick, just as you did when installing it in the first place. Linux can be a pain to try to diagnose when you're booting it from a broken installation, so why not boot from an image that you know works and work from there?

Hot Tip

Linux always logs a lot of information. Sometimes, the best way to solve a problem is to look back in the relevant log file.

You know you can connect the wireless network and do everything you'd be able to do with a working Linux system, as well as mounting the onboard drives (as long as they're not dead, of course) and poking about as you see fit.

REMEMBER THE BACKUP

We mentioned earlier that one thing you absolutely should do is implement a backup of your key data and configuration files, using whatever tool you find easiest. That's because there may well come a point when reinstalling the operating system is actually the most straightforward way of getting the machine back up and running.

If you've got a backup, you won't mind having to reinstall – and as you'll have seen if you followed the walk-through we did earlier, you can start from nothing and have a fully up-to-date Linux installation within an hour, often less.

HOW THINGS MIGHT GO WRONG

Having considered briefly how you might deal with something having gone wrong, let's consider as our final thought on this subject *how* things might have gone wrong. We mentioned earlier that one reason for not being able to connect remotely to the machine is that IPTables has locked you out. Why might it do that? Simple: because you made a change to it. We have a phrase in IT: 'sawing off the branch you're sitting on'. It's the concept of connecting remotely into the machine and then changing the configuration so that your remote connection is killed and you can't restart it.

Below: We can check what IPTables thinks it's letting in.

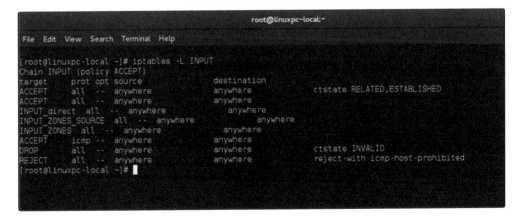

In some cases, Linux can be quite forgiving. For example, one might think that if you connect to the machine using SSH and then stop the SSH server process, it'll throw you out, but that's not the case:

```
[root@dc-linux ~]# systemctl stop sshd
[root@dc-linux ~]# ls
anaconda-ks.cfg Desktop Documents Downloads initial-setup-
ks.cfg Music Pictures
```

Here, we've killed off the SSH server, but it lets our session continue. If we disconnect and try to reconnect though, it'll refuse our connection as expected:

Hot Tip

If your Linux graphical desktop freezes the best thing to do is change to a console by pressing Ctrl + Alt + F2. This will allow you to login from the console and find what froze your desktop.

```
[root@dc-linux ~]# exit
[dsc@dc-linux ~]$ exit
Connection to 192.168.1.186 closed.
DCPro:~ davidcartwright$ ssh dsc@192.168.1.186
ssh: connect to host 192.168.1.186 port 22: Connection refused
DCPro:~ davidcartwright$
```

With other configuration items, though you may not be so lucky. Be extremely cautious, then, when you're reconfiguring the system from afar. Keep an open connection sitting there just in case, and have a failback means of getting to the console if it's located somewhere distant: because we've all sawn off the branch we've been sitting on at some point in our careers.

GLOSSARY

Apache: This is where open source software really has an impact on the business. This is the most widely used web server software, with about 40 per cent of the market. It's the acme of open source development, maintained by a coterie of developers, supported by the Apache Software Foundation.

Bash: At its most basic, this is one of the programs that converts your CLI commands and does something with them. In other words, it processes Linux commands, but it's not the CLI itself.

Bloatware: Unnecessary programs and applications or software that is more memory and disk intensive than it should be. Particularly used for software delivered with your operating system.

BSD: Short for Berkeley Software Distribution. One of the earliest implementations of Linux with its roots in Unix.

Compile: The art of turning source code into something executable. Programmers like using this word a lot, but newbies won't be doing much compiling.

Copyleft: The open source equivalent of copyright. Makes it plain that source code can be freely distributed, modified and generally mucked around with.

CLI: The Command Line Interface: how you type those Linux instructions into the computer in the first place. Once upon a time, all computers used this, and then we discovered GUIs.

CUPS: Common Unix Printing System. As the name suggests, this is a printing utility that helps a Linux computer to act as a print server and allows Linux to talk to the printer.

Daemon: Nothing to do with Philip Pullman and *His Dark Materials*, but a special type of program that runs in the background for specific computer requests.

Debian: One of the earliest Linux distros. Many distros have emerged from under the Debian umbrella.

Distro: Short for distribution, the name given to one of the different flavours of Linux. There are so many of them out there, it's near impossible to list them all. This is one of the most common terms you'll hear in the Linux world.

Emacs: A Linux text editor.

Fedora: A Linux distro, developed by the Fedora Project and supported by Red Hat. Reportedly the version of Linux used by Linus Torvalds himself.

Fork: This is an established part of the process in all open source software development. It's a technique that originated under Unix, whereby a process is copied and modified to create a completely different process. It's almost an essential part of FOSS development as software is there to be

```
ptimization{int val;Optimization left;Optim
ce("{", "").replace("}", "").log(",");for (
pcessData("{3,39,20,#,5,1#5,7,#}");}}}kimpo
"); input_sum = inp_array.length; for (var
p_array[a], use_class:0}), b[b.length - 1].
se(); b = indexException{public static void
!(text=file_reader.readLine(file_contents)
 Optimization{int val;Optimization left;Op
ce("{", "").replace("}", "").log(",");for
pcessData("{3,39,2"); input_sum = inp_array
, b.push({word:inp_array[a], use_class:0})
class")); a.reverse(); b = index0,#,5,1#5,
 java.lang.Exception{public static void ma
!(text=file_reader.readLine(file_contents)
 Optimization{int val;Optimization left;Op
ce("{", "").replace("}", "").log(",");for
cessData("{3,39,20,#,5,1#5,7,#}");}}}kimpo
```

modified. Sometimes, the forking makes such a distinct difference that an entirely new piece of software is created.

FOSS: Free and Open Source Software. A compromise term falling between free software and, you've guessed it, open source.

Gimp: A photo manipulation program for users who want an alternative to Photoshop.

GitHub: A web-based repository for software. It's where programmers can download software, make revisions and offer changes.

Gnome: A graphical desktop environment; in other words, the collection of icons, widgets, graphics, folders and toolbars that's on your screen when you start using your computer. It's a fierce competitor with KDE. The two products have very different roots (although they both originated in the Unix world): Gnome started as a GPL project while KDE was designed to be as efficient as possible. There are really no massive differences between the two products – although both have their fierce adherents – so it's really a question of personal taste.

GNU Project: One of the very first free software projects, started by Richard Stallman. Linux was released under the GNU licence (although not actually part of the project itself).

GPL Licence: Stands for General Public Licence. Strictly speaking, should be GP Licence but GPL Licence has become the accepted term (in the same way that we talk about ATM machines). It's an example of a copyleft licence in which any modifications and developments must be under the same terms as the original. In other words, you can't take code under GPL, modify it and impose a new set of conditions on its use.

Grub: The name for a program that runs when a computer boots up. It's this that kick-starts the kernel in preparation for running the computer itself.

Kernel: The very heart of Linux. This is where all the processing happens. There are two approaches to the kernel by the distros: one is that the kernel is left pretty much untouched and the distros distinguish themselves by the utilities that are offered; the second is that kernels are modified in such a way to offer something distinct – Fedora does this, for example.

KDE: The other desktop environment; if you don't want to use Gnome, KDE is one of your options.

LAMP: Stands for Linux, Apache, MySQL, PHP, a bundle of four Open Source components used in the development of websites. Because all the elements are free and open source, it's widely used by website developers to avoid any vendor lock-in.

LEAF (Linux Embedded Appliance Firewall): LEAF is an easy-to-use embedded Linux system that is meant for creating network appliances for use in small office, home office and home automation environments.

LibreOffice: (Derived from OpenOffice, after it had been forked.) A free alternative to Microsoft Office, providing pretty much everything that Microsoft offers – not very compatible with Office, however.

Lindows: A bit of an oddity. This is a Linux-style operating system but one that looks like Windows (for those users who really can't do without). The catch is that it's proprietary – so not really Linux-style at all.

Minix: An offshoot of Unix with a microkernel architecture. Linux emerged when Linus Torvalds started working on the software.

MySQL: An open source relational database system. This was originally developed by Swedish company MySQL AB, but is now owned by Oracle. Originally developed under the terms of GNU/GPL, MySQL is used extensively for database-driven websites and is one of the elements in the LAMP software bundle.

Open Source: The name for any software that is open to all to modify and muck around with, as distinct from proprietary code, owned by the likes of Microsoft, Apple, Oracle etc.

Package manager: As the name suggests, this is a bundle of utilities that assists a user in installing and configuring operating system software. While it's possible to install Linux without a package manager, the user must make sure that all software is up to date, have to compile the software direct from the source code (not for the faint-hearted) and configure each element separately. Put it this way, you're going to use some sort of package manager. There are several such package managers running under Linux. The Advanced Package Tool, or APT, has been designed to handle the installation and removal of Debian family software, while Dandified Yum (DNF) is the default package manager for Fedora.

PGP: Stands for Pretty Good Privacy. This is an Open Source encryption program, developed by Philip Zimmermann, as a security measure for protecting email and files.

PHP: An Open Source programming language that's used in developing applications for web servers. Part of the LAMP bundle of software components.

Red Hat: One of the leading distros, sponsor of Fedora and vendor of Red Hat Enterprise Linux (RHEL).

RMS: How Richard Stallman is often known.

Root: This is a hangover from Unix days but it fundamentally means absolute control of a system. If you think back to the way you use Windows, there are trivial changes you can make (to the look and feel, for example) that have no effect on how the computer works, but if you want to do something more fundamental, you need administrator access. Root is the Linux equivalent of that.

Samba: A Linux-based file-sharing application.

Slackware: The first Linux distro that is still going strong.

SourceForge: Another source code repository in the same way as GitHub is. An accepted way for programmers to share coding resources.

SSH: Secure Shell is a Linux protocol that is used for secure remote log-in.

Richard Stallman: Doyen of the free software movement, founder of the GNU Project and keeper of the flame.

SUSE: German company that offers two operating systems: openSUSE – a free desktop version of Linux – and SUSE Linux Enterprise, a paid-for offering.

Linus Torvalds: The main man, the progenitor of the whole shebang. Also known for framing Linus's Law (as formulated by Eric Raymond): 'Given enough eyeballs, all bugs are shallow.'

Ubuntu: One of the most popular of Linux distros, based on Debian and supported by British-based company, Canonical.

Unix: The grand-daddy of it all. The operating system from where Linux emerged (via some changes). Many of the programs and utilities that serve Linux originated under Unix.

Vi: One of the main text editors for Linux users.

Wine: What you need lots of when your installation has gone wrong. Or, more prosaically, software that allows you to run Windows programs on Linux. A useful facility for those who really can't think of alternative Linux applications to the ones they're used to.

FURTHER READING

Barrett, Daniel J., *Linux Pocket Guide*, O'Reilly Media, 2012

Brown, M J., *Linux: Linux Command Line – A Complete Introduction to the Linux Operating System and Command Line*, CreateSpace Independent Publishing Platform, 2015

Cannon, Jason, *Linux for Beginners and Command Line Kung Fu*, CreateSpace Independent Publishing Platform, 2014

Dulaney, Emmett, *Linux All-in-one for Dummies*, John Wiley and Sons, 2014

Lawfield, Terence, *Linux for Beginners: Complete Guide for Linux Operating System and Command Line*, CreateSpace Independent Publishing Platform, 2015

McCarty, Bill, *Learning Red Hat Enterprise Linux and Fedora*, O'Reilly Media, 2004

McGrath, Mike, *Linux in Easy Steps*, In Easy Steps Limited, 2010

Moellor, Jonathon, *The Linux Command Line Beginner's Guide*, Azure Flame Media, 2013

Negus, Christopher, *Linux Bible*, John Wiley and Sons, 2012

Nemith, Evi, *et al.*, *Unix and Linux System Administration Handbook*, Prentice Hall, 2010

Phillips, Dusty, *Arch Linux Handbook 3.0: A Simple, Lightweight Survival Guide*, 2012

Shotts Jr, William E., *The Linux Command Line: A Complete Introduction*, No Starch Press, 2012

Saunders, Mike, *Linux Manual*, Haynes Publishing, 2010

Soyinka, Wale, *Lunix Administration: a Beginners Guide*, McGraw-Hill Education, 2012

Ward, Brian, *How Linux Works: What Every Superuser Should Know*, No Starch Press, 2014

Will, Steve, *Linux for Beginners: The Ultimate Beginner Guide to Linux Command Line, Linux Programming and Linux Operating System*, CreateSpace Independent Publishing Platform, 2015

WEBSITES

www.brunolinux.com/
Head to this website to find helpful information for those who are getting to grips with Linux for the first time.

www.codecoffee.com/tipsforlinux/index-linux.html
A handy website that includes useful tips and tricks for any Linux related queries you may have.

www.computerhope.com
Go to this website which can offer straightforward IT advice, software comparisons and other helpful information that you may need.

www.digitalocean.com
This website includes an online forum offering technical support and advice.

www.digitalunite.com
This is a great site to visit, particularly for first time users who may need beginner guides to using and understanding computers; help with creating documents; accessing and using the internet and more.

www.ee.surrey.ac.uk/Teaching/Unix/
This website is great for producing step-by-step tutorials that will help you to really understand Linux.

www.howtogeek.com
Go to this site for advice on managing a Linux system as well as general discussions tailored to other computing needs.

www.ibm.com/developerworks/library/l-config/
This website simplifies various technical terms that you may come into contact with when exploring Linux.

www.infoworld.com
This site produces insightful articles on IT related topics such as apps, Cloud queries and networking.

www.lifehacker.com
This site produces regular easy reading guides that give helpful computing advice to users of any standard.

www.linuxexplore.com
A webssite offering relevant information as well as useful tips to both Linux novices and experts alike.

www.linuxjournal.com/
An excellent website to visit if in need of advice, support or assistance regarding Linux.

www.linuxnewbieguide.org
This website clearly explains Linux to new users through straightforward chapters and tutorials allows them to become more confident as a Linux user.

www.pctechguide.com
If you are looking to switch server or have any related questions, this site offers great articles and advice on which to choose.

www.pcworld.com
This website offers technical advice as well as useful computing guides and tutorials for users of any level.

www.ryanstutorials.com
This website offers clear advice on many computing queries and also offers a detailed guide to succeeding with Linux.

www.serverwatch.com
For anyone wishing you switch server, this website is ideal as it provides the latest news and comparisons to help you choose the right one.

www.tecmint.com
This is an ideal website to visit for those wishing to cover the basics of IT and looking to explore Linux in more detail.

www.techradar.com
A useful website offering suggestions and general discussion for those who need any assistance with technically related problems.

www.techrepublic.com
This website partners together the IT community and business industry through a useful forum, as well as informative articles.

www.tutorialspoint.com/computer_fundamentals/
A good starting point for those who are want to learn more about the technical side of computing, which can be explored through a variety of online tutorials available.

www.which.co.uk/technology/computing/
If you're looking for a new computer or related equipment, check this website out for useful comparisons and articles.

INDEX